CUMIN-SCENTED SWEET POTATO WEDGES, PAGE 71 AND ULTIMATE ONION RINGS, PAGE 68

## WEIGHT WATCHERS PUBLISHING GROUP

| | |
|---|---|
| EDITORIAL DIRECTOR | **NANCY GAGLIARDI** |
| CREATIVE DIRECTOR | **ED MELNITSKY** |
| PRODUCTION MANAGER | **ALAN BIEDERMAN** |
| PHOTO EDITOR | **DEBORAH HARDT** |
| MANAGING EDITOR | **SARAH WHARTON** |
| EDITORIAL ASSISTANT | **CELIA SHATZMAN** |
| FOOD EDITOR | **EILEEN RUNYAN** |
| EDITOR | **DEBORAH MINTCHEFF** |
| NUTRITION CONSULTANT | **U. BEATE KRINKE** |
| COVER PHOTOGRAPHER | **RITA MAAS** |
| COVER FOOD STYLIST | **ANNE DISRUDE** |
| COVER PROP STYLIST | **CATHY COOK** |
| PHOTOGRAPHER | **JAMES BAIGRIE** |
| FOOD STYLIST | **MICHAEL PEDERSON** |
| PROP STYLIST | **CATHY COOK** |
| ART DIRECTOR | **DANIELA HRITCU** |

ON THE COVER: Cumin-Scented Sweet Potato Wedges, page 71

# Hit the
# Spot

## 140
### Savory, Crispy, Spicy & Sweet Recipes You'll Love

# About Weight Watchers

Weight Watchers International, Inc. is the world's leading provider of weight-management services, operating globally through a network of Company-owned and franchise operations. Weight Watchers holds over 48,000 weekly meetings, where members receive group support and education about healthful eating patterns, behavior modification, and physical activity. Weight-loss and weight-management results vary by individual. We recommend that you attend Weight Watchers meetings to benefit from the supportive environment you'll find there and follow the comprehensive Weight Watchers program, which includes a food plan, an activity plan, and a behavioral component. In addition, Weight Watchers offers a wide range of products, publications and programs for those interested in weight loss and weight control. For the Weight Watchers meeting nearest you, call 1-800-651-6000. For information on bringing Weight Watchers to your workplace, call **1-800-8AT-WORK**. Also, visit us at our Web site, **WeightWatchers.com**, or look for *Weight Watchers Magazine* at your newsstand or in your meeting room.

# About Our Recipes

We make every effort to ensure that you will have success with our recipes. For best results and for nutritional accuracy, please keep these guidelines in mind:

• Recipes in this book have been developed for members who are following the Momentum™ plan. We include **POINTS**® values for every recipe. **POINTS** values are assigned based on calories, fat (grams), and fiber (grams) provided for a serving size of a recipe.

• All recipes feature approximate nutritional information; our recipes are analyzed for Calories (Cal), Total Fat (Fat), Saturated Fat (Sat Fat), Trans Fat (Trans Fat), Cholesterol (Chol), Sodium (Sod), Carbohydrates (Carb), Dietary Fiber (Fib), Protein (Prot), and Calcium (Calc).

• Nutritional information for recipes that include meat, poultry, and fish are based on cooked skinless boneless portions (unless otherwise stated), with the fat trimmed.

• We recommend that you buy lean meat and poultry, then trim it of all visible fat before cooking. When poultry is cooked with the skin on, we suggest removing the skin before eating.

• Before serving, divide foods—Including any vegetables, accompaniments, or sauces—into portions of equal size according to the designated number of servings per recipe.

• Any substitutions made to the ingredients will alter the "Per serving" nutritional information and may affect the **POINTS** value.

• All fresh fruits, vegetables, and greens in recipes should be rinsed before using.

• All ◆™ Filling Extra suggestions have a **POINTS** value of **0** unless otherwise stated.

**PORK AND TOMATO CARNITAS, PAGE 78**

# contents

# Simply
# Savory

chapter 1

# Tapas-Style Almonds

prep 5 min   cook 5 min   serve 6 as a light bite

½   teaspoon olive oil
½   cup whole blanched almonds
¼   teaspoon kosher salt
Pinch cayenne

Heat the oil in a small nonstick skillet over medium-high heat. Add the almonds and reduce the heat to medium-low. Cook, shaking the skillet occasionally, until the almonds just begin to brown, about 5 minutes. Immediately transfer the almonds to a serving bowl. Sprinkle with the salt and cayenne, tossing to coat. Serve warm or at room temperature.

PER SERVING (about 10 almonds): 73 Cal, 6 g Fat, 1 g Sat Fat, 0 g Trans Fat, 0 mg Chol, 65 mg Sod, 2 g Carb, 1 g Fib, 3 g Prot, 30 mg Calc. **POINTS** value: **2.**

## So Satisfying
These addictive salty, savory almonds are super-fast to make and the perfect finger food. Try them as a simple snack or as a delicious addition to a tapas menu.

# Bite-Size Blue Cheese Popovers

prep 10 min   bake 25 min   serves 6 as a light bite

| | |
|---|---|
| 6 | large egg whites |
| 1 | cup low-fat (1%) milk |
| ³/₄ | cup all-purpose flour |
| ¹/₄ | cup whole-wheat flour |
| 3 | tablespoons reduced-fat blue cheese, finely crumbled |
| 2 | tablespoons olive oil |
| 1 | tablespoon chopped fresh rosemary |
| ¹/₄ | teaspoon salt |

1 Preheat the oven to 400°F. Spray a 24-cup mini-muffin pan with nonstick spray.

2 Whisk the egg whites in a large bowl until frothy. Add the remaining ingredients and whisk just until the flour is no longer visible. Fill each muffin cup about three quarters full with the batter.

3 Bake the popovers until puffed and golden, about 25 minutes. Remove the popovers from the muffin cups. Serve hot.

PER SERVING (4 popovers): 158 Cal, 6 g Fat, 1 g Sat Fat, 0 g Trans Fat, 4 mg Chol, 220 mg Sod, 18 g Carb, 1 g Fib, 8 g Prot, 75 mg Calc. **POINTS** value: **3.**

## In the Kitchen

The batter can be made ahead and refrigerated, covered, for up to 2 days. Once completely cooled, the popovers can be placed in a large zip-close plastic freezer bag and frozen for up to 1 month. To warm the frozen popovers, put them on a baking sheet and place in a preheated 325°F oven until heated through, about 10 minutes.

# Overstuffed Avocado–BLT Pizza

prep 10 min   bake 10 min   serves 8 as a light bite

| | |
|---|---|
| 1 | (10-ounce) prebaked thin whole-wheat pizza crust |
| 3 | tablespoons reduced-fat mayonnaise |
| 2 | cups lightly packed mixed baby salad greens |
| 1 | tomato, diced |
| 1 | avocado, halved, pitted, peeled, and diced |
| 4 | slices turkey bacon, crisp cooked and coarsely crumbled |

1 Preheat the oven to 450°F.

2 Place the pizza crust on a baking sheet. Bake until crisp, about 10 minutes. Transfer the crust to a wire rack and let cool slightly.

3 Spread the mayonnaise evenly over the crust. Top with the remaining ingredients and cut into 8 wedges.

PER SERVING (1 wedge): 171 Cal, 8 g Fat, 2 g Sat Fat, 0 g Trans Fat, 9 mg Chol, 396 mg Sod, 20 g Carb, 4 g Fib, 7 g Prot, 61 mg Calc. **POINTS** value: **3.**

## So Satisfying

Crisp pieces of salty, smoky bacon and lots of ripe avocado enrich this quick pizza, made with a prebaked pizza crust filled with the goodness of whole wheat. Enjoy a wedge with a bowl of Potato-Vegetable Soup (page 15) and it becomes lunch. The **POINTS** value for each serving will increase by **3.**

**OVERSTUFFED AVOCADO–BLT PIZZA**

# Lemon-Dill Smoked Salmon with Fennel and Olives

prep 15 min   cook none   serve 6 as a light bite

| | |
|---|---|
| 1 | fennel bulb, thinly sliced |
| 1 | shallot, minced |
| 6 | pitted kalamata olives, chopped |
| 1 | tablespoon capers, drained |
| 1 | tablespoon chopped fresh dill |
| 2 | teaspoons lemon juice |
| 3 | (4-ounce) packages thinly sliced smoked salmon |

1 Toss together all the ingredients except the smoked salmon in a medium bowl.

2 Arrange the salmon, in one layer, on a round platter. Sprinkle evenly with the fennel mixture. Serve at once or cover with plastic wrap and refrigerate up to 2 hours.

PER SERVING (2$^1$/$_2$ slices salmon and $^1$/$_4$ cup fennel mixture): 87 Cal, 3 g Fat, 1 g Sat Fat, 0 g Trans Fat, 13 mg Chol, 543 mg Sod, 4 g Carb, 1 g Fib, 11 g Prot, 32 mg Calc. *POINTS* value: **2.**

## In the Kitchen
Using presliced smoked salmon makes this dish a snap to put together. Each package contains about 5 slices and is available in the seafood section of most supermarkets. This recipe works with the Simply Filling technique.

# Potato-Vegetable Soup

prep 10 min   microwave 20 min   serves 4

1   (½-pound) all-purpose potato,
    peeled and diced

1   onion, chopped

1   small tomato, chopped

2   garlic cloves, minced

2   teaspoons olive oil

1   zucchini, diced

1   (10-ounce) package frozen
    lima beans

¼   pound baby spinach, coarsely
    chopped

1   (32-ounce) carton reduced-
    sodium chicken broth

1 Combine the potato, onion, tomato, garlic, and oil in a large microwavable bowl. Cover with plastic wrap and vent one corner. Microwave on High until the potatoes are almost tender, about 10 minutes.

2 Add the zucchini, beans, spinach, and broth to the potato mixture. Microwave, covered, on High until the vegetables are very tender, about 10 minutes longer.

PER SERVING (1¾ cups): 188 Cal, 3 g Fat, 0 g Sat Fat, 0 g Trans Fat, 0 mg Chol, 608 mg Sod, 32 g Carb, 7 g Fib, 10 g Prot, 91 mg Calc. **POINTS** value: **3.**

## In the Kitchen
No need to thaw the lima beans. Once they hit the hot soup, they'll thaw. This recipe works with the Simply Filling technique.

**PARMESAN AND GARLIC–STUFFED MUSSELS AND TAPAS-STYLE ALMONDS, PAGE 10**

# Parmesan and Garlic–Stuffed Mussels

prep 10 min   cook/bake 10 min   serves 4 as a light bite

3    tablespoons plain dried
     whole-wheat bread crumbs

3    tablespoons grated Parmesan
     cheese

1    tablespoon chopped fresh
     parsley

1    tablespoon chopped fresh
     thyme or 1 teaspoon dried

2    garlic cloves, minced

2    teaspoons olive oil

16   mussels, scrubbed and
     debearded

1 Preheat the oven to 425°F.

2 Stir together all the ingredients except the mussels in a small bowl.

3 Fill a large saucepan with 1/2 inch of water and bring to a boil over high heat; add the mussels. Reduce the heat and simmer, covered, until the mussels open, about 5 minutes; drain. Discard any mussels that do not open.

4 When the mussels are cool enough to handle, remove and discard the top half of each shell. Arrange the mussels in their shells in a shallow baking pan. Spoon about 1 teaspoon of the bread crumb mixture over each mussel; lightly spray with olive oil nonstick spray. Bake until the mussels are cooked through and the topping is golden, about 10 minutes.

PER SERVING (4 stuffed mussels): 116 Cal, 5 g Fat, 1 g Sat Fat, 0 g Trans Fat, 25 mg Chol, 305 mg Sod, 6 g Carb, 1 g Fib, 11 g Prot, 108 mg Calc. **POINTS** value: **3.**

◆ Filling Extra

For a tempting antipasto platter, serve these cheesy, garlicky mussels on a platter with jarred roasted bell peppers (not oil packed), sprinkled with chopped fresh basil and some thickly sliced white mushrooms, sprinkled with black pepper.

# Creamy Minted Pea Soup

prep 5 min   microwave/cook 15 min   serves 4

| | |
|---|---|
| 1 | onion, chopped |
| 1 | garlic clove, minced |
| 2 | teaspoons olive oil |
| 1 | (10-ounce) package frozen peas |
| 1 | (32-ounce) carton reduced- sodium chicken broth |
| 2 | tablespoons fat-free half-and-half |
| 2 | tablespoons chopped fresh mint |

1 Combine the onion, garlic, and oil in a large microwavable bowl. Cover with plastic wrap and vent one corner. Microwave on High until the onion is softened, about 5 minutes. Add the peas and broth. Microwave, covered, on High until the peas are tender and the soup just begins to boil, about 5 minutes longer. Stir in the half-and-half. Let the soup cool about 5 minutes.

2 Puree the soup, in batches if necessary, in a blender. Stir in the mint. If serving the soup hot, transfer to a large saucepan and cook over medium heat until heated through, about 5 minutes. Or refrigerate, covered, and serve chilled.

PER SERVING (1 1/3 cups): 102 Cal, 3 g Fat, 0 g Sat Fat, 0 g Trans Fat, 0 mg Chol, 581 mg Sod, 13 g Carb, 3 g Fib, 7 g Prot, 50 mg Calc. **POINTS** value: **2.**

◆ Filling Extra

To make this delicate soup a little heartier, add a 15½-ounce can of cannellini (white kidney) beans, rinsed and drained, to the pureed soup. Or, to retain the soup's creamy texture, puree the beans with ½ cup of the soup liquid, then stir the mixture into the soup. The **POINTS** value for each serving will increase by **1.**

# Super-Fast Asparagus with Orange Mayonnaise

prep 10 min   microwave 5 min   serves 4

1   **(1-pound) bunch asparagus, trimmed**

¼   **cup water**

½   **cup fat-free mayonnaise**

1   **tablespoon grated orange zest**

2   **tablespoons orange juice**

1   **tablespoon lemon juice**

1   **tablespoon finely chopped fresh parsley**

½   **teaspoon honey**

1   **garlic clove, minced**

1 Place the asparagus in a large microwavable dish. Cover with plastic wrap and vent one corner. Microwave on High until crisp-tender, about 3 minutes; drain. Arrange the spears on a platter. Let cool, if desired.

2 To prepare the orange mayonnaise, stir together the remaining ingredients in a small bowl. Spoon the mayonnaise over the asparagus.

PER SERVING (about 5 asparagus and 2½ tablespoons mayonnaise): 44 Cal, 1 g Fat, 1 g Sat Fat, 0 g Trans Fat, 3 mg Chol, 243 mg Sod, 9 g Carb, 2 g Fib, 2 g Prot, 23 mg Calc. **POINTS** value: **1.**

## In the Kitchen

To ensure even cooking in the microwave, arrange the asparagus spears so that their tips face the center of the dish.

# Fresh Corn Salad with Heirloom Tomatoes and Lime

prep 20 min   cook none   serves 4

| | |
|---|---|
| 2 | cups fresh corn kernels (from about 2 ears of corn) |
| 2 | small tomatoes, preferably heirloom, diced |
| 3 | scallions, chopped |
| 3 | tablespoons chopped fresh mint |
| 1 | jalapeño pepper, seeded and minced |
| 1 | garlic clove, minced |
| 2 | tablespoons lime juice |
| 2 | teaspoons extra-virgin olive oil |
| ½ | teaspoon salt |

Toss together all the ingredients in a serving bowl. Serve at once or cover and refrigerate up to 2 hours.

PER SERVING (¾ cup): 90 Cal, 3 g Fat, 0 g Sat Fat, 0 g Trans Fat, 0 mg Chol, 309 mg Sod, 16 g Carb, 3 g Fib, 2 g Prot, 19 mg Calc. **POINTS** value: **1.**

## In the Kitchen

If you use tender sweet corn there is no need to cook it. But if you prefer your corn cooked, put the kernels in a small microwavable dish. Cover the dish with plastic wrap and vent one corner. Microwave on High until the corn is tender, about 4 minutes. Let cool. **This recipe works with the Simply Filling technique.**

**FRESH CORN SALAD WITH HEIRLOOM TOMATOES AND LIME**

# Grilled Peppers with Black Olives and Goat Cheese

prep 15 min   grill 10 min   serves 4

| | |
|---|---|
| 4 | large bell peppers |
| 1 | garlic clove |
| 3 | tablespoons chopped fresh basil |
| 1 | tablespoon olive oil |
| ¼ | teaspoon salt |
| 3 | tablespoons reduced-fat soft (mild) goat cheese, crumbled |
| 6 | oil-cured black olives, pitted and coarsely chopped |

1 Spray the grill rack with nonstick spray. Preheat the grill to medium-high or prepare a medium-high fire.

2 Place the bell peppers on the grill rack and grill, turning occasionally, until the peppers are softened and the skins are blackened, about 10 minutes. Put the peppers in a large zip-close plastic bag; squeeze out the air and seal the bag. Let steam 10 minutes.

3 Meanwhile, with the side of a large knife, mash the garlic until it forms a paste.

4 When the peppers are cool enough to handle, slip off the skins and remove the stems and seeds; discard. Cut the flesh lengthwise into 1-inch strips.

5 Toss together the peppers, basil, oil, garlic, and salt in a large bowl. Pile the peppers on a platter. Sprinkle with the goat cheese and olives. Let stand at least 15 minutes or up to 1 hour to allow the flavors to develop.

PER SERVING (½ cup): 89 Cal, 6 g Fat, 2 g Sat Fat, 0 g Trans Fat, 3 mg Chol, 229 mg Sod, 8 g Carb, 3 g Fib, 3 g Prot, 35 mg Calc. **POINTS** value: **2.**

## So Satisfying

The combination of freshly grilled fleshy bell peppers, soft, tangy goat cheese, and salty black olives is sure to have 'em wanting seconds. Serve these peppers as a side dish, add them to an antipasto platter, or pile them on top of a chicken or turkey sandwich as a flavor-packed add-on.

# Lemon-Basil Mashed Potatoes

prep 15 min   cook 20 min   serves 4

1¼ pounds baby red potatoes, scrubbed and halved

½ cup reduced-sodium chicken broth, warmed

1 tablespoon unsalted butter

½ teaspoon salt

¼ teaspoon black pepper

2 tablespoons chopped fresh basil

1 tablespoon grated lemon zest

2 teaspoons lemon juice

1 Put the potatoes in a medium saucepan and add enough water to cover; bring to a boil over high heat. Reduce the heat and simmer until the potatoes are tender, about 20 minutes; drain.

2 Return the potatoes to the saucepan. Add the broth, butter, salt, and pepper. Mash until the potatoes are smooth. Stir in the basil and lemon zest and juice.

PER SERVING (¾ cup): 136 Cal, 3 g Fat, 2 g Sat Fat, 0 g Trans Fat, 8 mg Chol, 374 mg Sod, 26 g Carb, 4 g Fib, 3 g Prot, 38 mg Calc. **POINTS** value: **2.**

◆ Filling Extra
Instead of the basil, stir in about 1 cup of cooked chopped spinach.

# Crispy Asian Slaw with Blender Peanut Sauce

prep 15 min    cook none    serves 4

3    tablespoons unseasoned rice vinegar

2    tablespoons reduced-sodium soy sauce

2    tablespoons reduced-fat creamy peanut butter

1    tablespoon coarsely chopped peeled fresh ginger

1    tablespoon packed brown sugar

1/2    head Savoy cabbage, thinly sliced (about 5 cups)

1    red bell pepper, cut into thin strips

1    cup packaged matchstick-cut carrots

1/4    cup chopped fresh cilantro

2    scallions, thinly sliced

1 To make the dressing, combine the vinegar, soy sauce, peanut butter, ginger, and brown sugar in a blender and puree.

2 Toss together the remaining ingredients in a serving bowl. Drizzle with the dressing and toss to coat evenly.

PER SERVING (1 1/4 cups): 117 Cal, 3 g Fat, 1 g Sat Fat, 0 g Trans Fat, 0 mg Chol, 365 mg Sod, 19 g Carb, 5 g Fib, 5 g Prot, 58 mg Calc. **POINTS** value: **2.**

◆ Filling Extra

Add more crunch and color to the slaw with a yellow or orange bell pepper, cut into thin strips.

# Cumin-Scented Snap Pea and Radish Salad

prep 10 min   cook none   serves 4

1   **pound sugar snap peas, trimmed**

1   **bunch radishes, trimmed and quartered**

1   **tablespoon unseasoned rice vinegar**

2   **teaspoons olive oil**

½   **teaspoon ground cumin**

¼   **teaspoon salt**

¼   **cup reduced-fat soft (mild) goat cheese, crumbled**

1 Combine the snap peas and radishes in a large bowl.

2 To make the dressing, whisk together the vinegar, oil, cumin, and salt in a small bowl. Drizzle the dressing over the vegetables and toss to coat evenly. Divide the salad evenly among 4 bowls or plates and sprinkle with the goat cheese.

PER SERVING (1 cup): 92 Cal, 4 g Fat, 2 g Sat Fat, 0 g Trans Fat, 4 mg Chol, 189 mg Sod, 9 g Carb, 3 g Fib, 5 g Prot, 64 mg Calc. **POINTS** value: **2.**

## So Satisfying

This salad takes advantage of one of summer's sweetest greens—sugar snap peas. Crisp sugar snaps and crunchy, peppery radishes pair perfectly with creamy mild goat cheese in this ideal warm-weather supper starter. If your radishes come with fresh-looking green tops, coarsely chop a handful and add to the salad.

**LEMON AND HERB–DRESSED ZUCCHINI AND ARUGULA SALAD**

# Lemon and Herb–Dressed Zucchini and Arugula Salad

prep 10 min   cook none   serves 2

1    cup lightly packed baby arugula
1    zucchini, sliced
2    teaspoons grated lemon zest
1    tablespoon lemon juice
1    teaspoon olive oil
¼    teaspoon salt
¼    teaspoon coarse black pepper
2    tablespoons thinly sliced fresh basil

1 Toss together the arugula and zucchini in a serving bowl.

2 To make the dressing, whisk together all the remaining ingredients except the basil in a small bowl. Drizzle the dressing over the arugula mixture and toss to coat evenly. Sprinkle with the basil.

PER SERVING (about 1 cup): 42 Cal, 3 g Fat, 0 g Sat Fat, 0 g Trans Fat, 0 mg Chol, 309 mg Sod, 5 g Carb, 2 g Fib, 2 g Prot, 41 mg Calc. **POINTS** value: **1.**

◆ Filling Extra
Serve this refreshing side dish with grilled chicken breasts (a 4-ounce grilled skinless, bone-in chicken breast brushed with 1 tablespoon barbecue sauce per serving will increase the **POINTS** value by **4**). This recipe works with the Simply Filling technique.

# Charred Summer Tomatoes
# with Feta and Herbs

prep 10 min   broil 10 min   serves 4

| | |
|---|---|
| 8 | small plum tomatoes (about 1 pound), halved lengthwise |
| 1 | tablespoon chopped fresh rosemary |
| 1–2 | teaspoons fennel seeds, crushed |
| 2 | teaspoons extra-virgin olive oil |
| ½ | teaspoon salt |
| ½ | teaspoon black pepper |
| ¼ | cup crumbled reduced-fat feta cheese |
| 1 | tablespoon chopped fresh oregano |

1 Spray the broiler rack with nonstick spray and preheat the broiler.

2 Toss together the tomatoes, rosemary, fennel seeds, oil, salt, and pepper in a large bowl. Arrange the tomatoes, cut side up, on the broiler rack. Broil 6 inches from the heat until the tomatoes are tender and lightly charred, about 5 minutes on each side.

3 Transfer the tomatoes to a platter; sprinkle with the feta and oregano. Serve hot, warm, or at room temperature.

PER SERVING (4 tomato halves): 65 Cal, 4 g Fat, 1 g Sat Fat, 0 g Trans Fat, 3 mg Chol, 410 mg Sod, 7 g Carb, 2 g Fib, 3 g Prot, 70 mg Calc. **POINTS** value: **1.**

◆ Filling Extra
Serve the tomatoes atop whole-wheat penne or spaghetti (1 cup cooked whole-wheat pasta for each serving will increase the **POINTS** value by **3**).

# Watercress-Tomato Salad with Blue Cheese Dressing

prep 15 min   cook none   serves 4

2   tablespoons reduced-fat blue cheese, crumbled

2   tablespoons cider vinegar

1   tablespoon extra-virgin olive oil

¼   teaspoon salt

¼   teaspoon black pepper

2   bunches watercress, trimmed

1   cup cherry tomatoes, halved

½   red onion, thinly sliced

To make the dressing, whisk together the blue cheese, vinegar, oil, salt, and pepper in a serving bowl. Add the watercress, tomatoes, and onion; toss to coat evenly.

PER SERVING (1½ cups salad): 59 Cal, 4 g Fat, 1 g Sat Fat, 0 g Trans Fat, 2 mg Chol, 209 mg Sod, 4 g Carb, 1 g Fib, 2 g Prot, 59 mg Calc. **POINTS** value: **1.**

◆ Filling Extra

Turn this side salad into a heartier offering—or light lunch—by adding slices of filet mignon or flank steak (3 ounces cooked filet mignon or flank steak, trimmed, for each serving will increase the **POINTS** value by **4**).

# Grilled Tri-Tip with Chipotle Butter–Slathered Corn

prep 15 min   grill 10 min   serves 4

| | |
|---|---|
| 1 | **(1-pound) tri-tip roast, trimmed** |
| ³/₄ | **teaspoon salt** |
| 4 | **ears of corn, husks and silk removed** |
| 2 | **tablespoons light stick butter, softened** |
| 1 | **tablespoon chopped fresh cilantro** |
| 1 | **tablespoon grated lime zest** |
| 1 | **teaspoon minced chipotle en adobo** |

1 Spray the grill rack with nonstick spray. Preheat the grill to medium-high or prepare a medium-high fire.

2 Sprinkle the beef with 1/2 teaspoon of the salt. Place the beef and corn on the grill rack. Grill the beef until an instant-read thermometer inserted into the center of the roast registers 145°F for medium-rare, about 10 minutes; grill the corn until lightly charred in spots and tender, about 10 minutes. Transfer the beef to a cutting board and let rest 10 minutes. Transfer the corn to a serving dish and keep warm.

3 Meanwhile, to make the chipotle butter, mash together the butter, cilantro, lime zest, chipotle en adobo, and the remaining 1/4 teaspoon salt in cup.

4 Cut the beef into 12 slices. Spread the chipotle butter over the corn and serve with the beef.

PER SERVING (3 slices beef, 1 ear corn, and about 2 teaspoons chipotle butter): 307 Cal, 8 g Fat, 3 g Sat Fat, 0 g Trans Fat, 86 mg Chol, 545 mg Sod, 25 g Carb, 4 g Fib, 35 g Prot, 9 mg Calc. **POINTS** value: **6.**

◆ Filling Extra

Round out this very summery meal with a plate of thickly sliced ripe tomatoes sprinkled with balsamic vinegar, dried oregano, salt, and pepper.

# Spice-Rubbed Mango-Glazed Pork Tenderloin

prep 10 min   grill 20 min   serves 4

¼  cup mango chutney
1  tablespoon dark rum
2  teaspoons cinnamon
½  teaspoon ground allspice
¾  teaspoon salt
1  (1-pound) pork tenderloin, trimmed

1 Spray the grill rack with nonstick spray. Preheat the grill to medium-high or prepare a medium-high fire.

2 To make the glaze, stir together the chutney and rum in a cup.

3 To make the rub, combine the cinnamon, allspice, and salt in a cup. Spread the rub all over the pork, then lightly spray with nonstick spray. Place the tenderloin on the grill rack and grill, turning, 10 minutes.

4 Continue to grill the pork, turning and brushing with the glaze, until an instant-read thermometer inserted into the center of the pork registers 160°F for medium, about 10 minutes longer. Transfer to a cutting board and let rest 5 minutes. Cut into 12 slices.

PER SERVING (3 slices pork): 186 Cal, 5 g Fat, 2 g Sat Fat, 0 g Trans Fat, 72 mg Chol, 503 mg Sod, 6 g Carb, 1 g Fib, 26 g Prot, 23 mg Calc. **POINTS** value: **4.**

◆ Filling Extra
Steamed spinach and creamy baked sweet potatoes make the perfect sides for this tenderloin (1 baked large sweet potato for each serving will increase the **POINTS** value by **3**).

# Peppered Sirloin with Black Bean, Tomato, and Avocado Salad

prep 15 min   cook 10 min   serves 4

| | |
|---|---|
| 1 | (1-pound) boneless sirloin steak, trimmed |
| 3/4 | teaspoon salt |
| 3/4 | teaspoon black pepper |
| 1 | (15½-ounce) can black beans, rinsed and drained |
| 1 | cup frozen corn kernels, thawed |
| 12 | grape tomatoes, halved |
| 1/2 | Hass avocado, halved, pitted, peeled, and cut into 1/2-inch pieces |
| 1 | jalapeño pepper, seeded and minced |
| 2 | tablespoons lime juice |
| 2 | teaspoons olive oil |
| 2 | tablespoons chopped fresh cilantro |

1 Sprinkle the steak with 1/2 teaspoon of the salt and the pepper. Spray a nonstick ridged grill pan with nonstick spray and set over medium-high heat. Place the steak on the pan and cook until an instant-read thermometer inserted into the center of the steak registers 145°F for medium-rare, about 5 minutes on each side. Transfer the steak to a cutting board and let rest 5 minutes.

2 Meanwhile, to make the salad, toss together the beans, corn, tomatoes, avocado, jalapeño, lime juice, oil, cilantro, and the remaining 1/4 teaspoon salt in a serving bowl.

3 Cut the steak into 12 slices and serve with the salad.

PER SERVING (3 slices steak and 3/4 cup salad): 355 Cal, 10 g Fat, 2 g Sat Fat, 0 g Trans Fat, 73 mg Chol, 771 mg Sod, 30 g Carb, 10 g Fib, 37 g Prot, 64 mg Calc. **POINTS** value: **7.**

◆ Filling Extra
Serve this salad on a bed of room-temperature whole-wheat couscous (2/3 cup cooked whole-wheat couscous for each serving will increase the **POINTS** value by **2**).
This recipe works with the Simply Filling technique.

**PEPPERED SIRLOIN WITH BLACK BEAN, TOMATO, AND AVOCADO SALAD**

# Penne with Asparagus, Ham, and Basil

prep 15 min   cook 20 min   serves 4

2   cups whole-wheat penne

2   teaspoons olive oil

1   large tomato, coarsely chopped

3   garlic cloves, thinly sliced

¹/₄   teaspoon red pepper flakes

1   (1-pound) bunch asparagus, trimmed and cut into 2-inch lengths

1   cup reduced-sodium chicken broth

1   tablespoon lemon juice

1   (¹/₂-pound) piece deli ham, cut into bite-size pieces

¹/₄   cup chopped fresh basil

3   tablespoons grated Parmesan cheese

1 Prepare the pasta according to the package directions, omitting the salt if desired; drain.

2 Meanwhile, heat the oil in a large nonstick skillet over medium-high heat. Add the tomato, garlic, and red pepper flakes; cook, stirring occasionally, until the tomato is softened, about 5 minutes. Add the asparagus, broth, and lemon juice; bring to a boil. Reduce the heat and simmer until the asparagus is tender, about 3 minutes longer.

3 Add the pasta, ham, basil, and Parmesan to the skillet; toss to combine.

**PER SERVING** (about 1³/₄ cups): 298 Cal, 8 g Fat, 2 g Sat Fat, 0 g Trans Fat, 34 mg Chol, 1060 mg Sod, 37 g Carb, 5 g Fib, 23 g Prot, 116 mg Calc. **POINTS** value: **6.**

## In the Kitchen

If you happen to have an herb garden—in a window box or outdoors—snip a handful of your favorite blend of herbs and toss into the skillet in step 3.

# Garlicky Chicken Kebabs with Fennel-Spiced Couscous

prep 15 min   cook/broil 15 min   serves 4

| | |
|---|---|
| 1 | cup reduced-sodium chicken broth |
| 1 | tablespoon lime juice |
| 1 | cup whole-wheat couscous |
| 2 | tablespoons chopped fresh cilantro |
| 2 | teaspoons grated lime zest |
| 1½ | pounds skinless boneless chicken breasts, cut into 1½-inch chunks |
| 3 | garlic cloves, minced |
| 1½ | tablespoons fennel seeds, crushed |
| 2 | teaspoons olive oil |
| ½ | teaspoon salt |

1 Spray the broiler rack with nonstick spray and preheat the broiler.

2 Bring the broth and lime juice to a boil in a medium saucepan; add the couscous, cilantro, and lime zest. Remove the saucepan from the heat. Let stand, covered, 5 minutes, then fluff with a fork; keep warm.

3 Combine the remaining ingredients in a medium bowl and toss to coat the chicken evenly. Thread the chicken on 4 (10- to 12-inch) metal skewers (if using wooden skewers, soak in water 30 minutes) dividing it evenly. Place the skewers on the broiler rack and broil 5 inches from the heat, turning occasionally, until the chicken is cooked through, about 8 minutes. Serve with the couscous.

PER SERVING (1 kebab and ¾ cup couscous): 321 Cal, 9 g Fat, 2 g Sat Fat, 0 g Trans Fat, 106 mg Chol, 533 mg Sod, 17 g Carb, 3 g Fib, 42 g Prot, 62 mg Calc. **POINTS** value: **7.**

◆ Filling Extra

All manner of vegetables can be added to the flavorful couscous after it is fluffed: a handful of halved cherry tomatoes, steamed diced zucchini, steamed small broccoli florets, or chopped roasted bell pepper. This recipe works with the Simply Filling technique.

**LAMB CHOPS WITH TOMATO-BELL PEPPER SALAD AND BULGUR**

# Lamb Chops with Tomato–Bell Pepper Salad and Bulgur

prep 10 min    cook 10 min    serves 4

1    cup grape tomatoes, halved

1    cup jarred roasted yellow bell pepper (not oil packed), drained and cut into 1/2-inch pieces

1    shallot, minced

2    tablespoons chopped fresh parsley

2    tablespoons chopped fresh chives

1    tablespoon capers, drained

2    teaspoons grated orange zest

1    tablespoon cider vinegar

2    teaspoons olive oil

3/4    teaspoon salt

1/2    teaspoon black pepper

1    cup bulgur

4    (1/4-pound)  lamb rib chops, about 3/4 inch thick, trimmed

1 To prepare the salad, combine the tomatoes, bell pepper, shallot, parsley, chives, capers, orange zest, vinegar, oil, 1/4 teaspoon of the salt and 1/4 teaspoon of the black pepper in a serving bowl.

2 Prepare the bulgur according to the package directions, omitting the salt and fat if desired.

3 Sprinkle the lamb with the remaining 1/2 teaspoon salt and 1/4 teaspoon black pepper. Spray a large nonstick ridged grill pan with nonstick spray and set over medium-high heat. Place the chops on the pan and cook, turning occasionally, until an instant-read thermometer inserted into the side of a chop registers 145°F for medium-rare, about 8 minutes. Place a chop on each of 4 plates. Divide the bulgur and salad evenly among the plates.

PER SERVING (1 lamb chop, 1 cup bulgur, and 1/2 cup salad): 256 Cal, 8 g Fat, 2 g Sat Fat, 0 g Trans Fat, 34 mg Chol, 646 mg Sod, 33 g Carb, 8 g Fib, 15 g Prot, 41 mg Calc. **POINTS** value: **5**.

## In the Kitchen

With their mild, sweet flavor and vibrant color, roasted yellow peppers are a great pantry item to have on hand. Use them to enhance any recipe or serve as a side dish or an easy appetizer. Roasted yellow peppers come packed in 16-ounce jars. This recipe works with the Simply Filling Technique.

# Roast Chicken Salad with Minted Summer Greens

prep 20 min   cook none   serves 4

| | |
|---|---|
| 1 | zucchini, halved lengthwise and sliced |
| ¹/₂ | cup lightly packed fresh mint leaves, torn if large |
| 1 | tablespoon lemon juice |
| 2 | teaspoons extra-virgin olive oil |
| ¹/₂ | teaspoon salt |
| ¹/₄ | teaspoon black pepper |
| 8 | cups mixed baby salad greens |
| 3 | cups shredded roast chicken breast (about 14 ounces) |

Combine the zucchini, mint, lemon juice, oil, salt, and pepper in a serving bowl. Let stand at least 5 minutes or up to 15 minutes. Add the salad greens and chicken; toss gently to mix well.

PER SERVING (about 2¹/₂ cups): 225 Cal, 7 g Fat, 2 g Sat Fat, 0 g Trans Fat, 86 mg Chol, 496 mg Sod, 6 g Carb, 3 g Fib, 34 g Prot, 84 mg Calc. **POINTS** value: **4.**

## So Satisfying

Bursting with flavor, this very summery main-dish salad is perfect for a crowd, as it requires no last-minute cooking and is ready in just 20 minutes. Plan ahead and roast a couple of chicken breasts a day or so ahead. **This recipe works with the Simply Filling technique.**

# Rosemary-Rubbed Salmon with Kalamata Olive Topping

prep 10 min    microwave 5 min    serves 4

4    (¹/₄-pound) skinless salmon
     fillets

1    tablespoon chopped fresh
     rosemary

¹/₂  teaspoon salt

¹/₄  cup pitted kalamata olives,
     chopped

¹/₄  cup dry-packed moist sun-dried
     tomatoes, chopped

3    tablespoons chopped fresh
     parsley

1¹/₂ teaspoons grated lemon zest

1¹/₂ teaspoons grated orange zest

1    garlic clove, minced

1    teaspoon olive oil

1 Sprinkle the salmon with the rosemary and salt. Spray a shallow 2-quart microwavable dish with nonstick spray. Place the salmon in the dish in one layer. Cover with plastic wrap and vent one corner. Microwave on High until the fish is just opaque in the center, about 5 minutes. Let rest 5 minutes.

2 Meanwhile, to make the topping, combine the remaining ingredients in a small bowl. Spoon the olive mixture over the salmon.

PER SERVING (1 salmon fillet and 2 tablespoons topping): 193 Cal, 9 g Fat, 2 g Sat Fat, 0 g Trans Fat, 75 mg Chol, 505 mg Sod, 3 g Carb, 1 g Fib, 25 g Prot, 33 mg Calc. *POINTS* value: **4.**

◆ Filling Extra
Round out this meal by serving baked potatoes alongside the fish (1 baked large potato for each serving will increase the *POINTS* value by **3**). This recipe works with the Simply Filling technique.

# Coconut and Curry–Marinated Skewered Chicken

prep 30 min   cook/grill 50 min   serves 4

| | |
|---|---|
| 1 | cup brown basmati rice |
| 1/3 | cup light coconut milk |
| 1 | tablespoon packed brown sugar |
| 1 | tablespoon lime juice |
| 1 | tablespoon garam masala |
| 1 | teaspoon Thai red curry paste |
| 1/2 | teaspoon salt |
| 1 | pound skinless boneless chicken thighs, trimmed and cut into 1 1/2-inch chunks |
| 3 | assorted color bell peppers, cut into 2-inch pieces |
| 3 | tablespoons unsweetened shredded coconut, toasted. |

1 Cook the rice according to the package directions, omitting the salt if desired.

2 Meanwhile, spray the grill rack with nonstick spray. Preheat the grill to medium-high or prepare a medium-high fire.

3 Combine the coconut milk, brown sugar, lime juice, garam masala, curry paste, and salt in a large bowl; add the chicken and toss until coated evenly. Alternately thread the chicken and bell peppers on 4 (10- to 12-inch) metal skewers dividing it evenly (if using wooden skewers soak in water 30 minutes). Place the skewers on the grill rack and grill, turning occasionally, until the chicken is cooked through and the vegetables are tender, about 10 minutes. Serve over the rice sprinkled with the coconut.

PER SERVING (1 skewer and 3/4 cup rice): 433 Cal, 14 g Fat, 6 g Sat Fat, 0 g Trans Fat, 70 mg Chol, 377 mg Sod, 47 g Carb, 8 g Fib, 29 g Prot, 63 mg Calc. **POINTS** value: **9.**

◆ Filling Extra
Serve with steamed halved baby bok choy.

**COCONUT AND CURRY–MARINATED SKEWERED CHICKEN**

# Striped Bass with Sweet Pepper Sauce

prep 10 min  cook 10 min  serves 4

| | |
|---|---|
| 1 | (7-ounce) jar roasted red pepper (not oil packed), drained |
| 1 | tablespoon balsamic vinegar |
| 2 | garlic cloves, coarsely chopped |
| ³/₄ | teaspoon salt |
| 3 | tablespoons chopped fresh basil |
| 4 | (6-ounce) striped bass fillets |
| ¹/₂ | teaspoon black pepper |
| 2 | teaspoons olive oil |

1 To make the sauce, combine the roasted peppers, vinegar, garlic, and ¹/₄ teaspoon of the salt in a blender or food processor and puree. Scrape the mixture into a small saucepan and set over medium heat. Cook, stirring frequently, until the sauce just begins to simmer. Remove from the heat and stir in the basil. Keep warm.

2 Sprinkle the bass fillets with the remaining ¹/₂ teaspoon salt and the black pepper. Heat the oil in a large nonstick skillet over medium-high heat. Add the fillets and cook until the fish is just opaque in the center, about 4 minutes on each side. Serve with the sauce.

PER SERVING (1 bass fillet and 2 tablespoons sauce): 236 Cal, 9 g Fat, 2 g Sat Fat, 0 g Trans Fat, 84 mg Chol, 615 mg Sod, 4 g Carb, 1 g Fib, 33 g Prot, 53 mg Calc. **POINTS** value: **5.**

◆ Filling Extra

For a satisfying side dish, serve this fish with baby potatoes sprinkled with salt and pepper to taste (two 2¹/₂-ounce cooked potatoes for each serving will increase the **POINTS** value by **2**). This recipe works with the Simply Filling Technique.

# Marseilles-Style Fish Soup

prep 40 min   cook 30 min   serves 4

| | |
|---|---|
| 1 | pound cod fillets, cut into 1-inch chunks |
| 2 | tablespoons Pernod |
| 2 | teaspoons grated orange zest |
| 2 | teaspoons olive oil |
| 2 | small leeks, cleaned and thinly sliced |
| 2 | small celery stalks, thinly sliced |
| 3 | garlic cloves, minced |
| 1 | tomato, chopped |
| 1 | (32-ounce) carton seafood broth or 4 (8-ounce) bottles clam juice |
| 1/2 | cup dry white wine |
| 1 | tablespoon harissa |
| 1/2 | teaspoon saffron threads, crushed |
| 1/2 | teaspoon herbes de Provence or dried thyme |

1 Combine the cod, Pernod, and orange zest in a large zip-close plastic bag. Squeeze out the air and seal the bag. Refrigerate at least 30 minutes or up to 2 hours, turning the bag occasionally.

2 Meanwhile, heat the oil in a large nonstick Dutch oven over medium-high heat. Add the leeks, celery, and garlic; cook, stirring occasionally, until golden, about 8 minutes. Add the tomato and cook, stirring occasionally, until softened, about 5 minutes. Stir in the remaining ingredients and bring to a boil. Reduce the heat and simmer until the flavors are blended, about 10 minutes longer.

3 Add the cod to the Dutch oven and bring to a boil over medium-high heat. Reduce the heat and gently simmer, covered, until the cod is just opaque in the center, about 5 minutes.

PER SERVING (2 cups): 200 Cal, 4 g Fat, 1 g Sat Fat, 0 g Trans Fat, 67 mg Chol, 678 mg Sod, 12 g Carb, 2 g Fib, 24 g Prot, 90 mg Calc. **POINTS** value: **4.**

## In the Kitchen
Pernod (PEHR-noh) is a delicate anise-flavored liqueur that is a classic ingredient in this Mediterranean favorite. Harissa, a fiery hot sauce from Tunisia, adds just the right amount of punch. It can be found in supermarkets and in specialty-foods stores.

**JERK SHRIMP WITH GINGERY PINEAPPLE SALSA**

# Jerk Shrimp with Gingery Pineapple Salsa

prep 10 min   broil 5 min   serves 4

1   (20-ounce) can crushed pineapple, drained

2   tablespoons minced red onion

2   tablespoons chopped fresh cilantro

2   tablespoons lime juice

1   tablespoon grated peeled fresh ginger

1   jalapeño pepper, seeded and minced

1   teaspoon honey

1   pound medium shrimp, peeled and deveined, tails left on if desired

1   tablespoon jerk seasoning

2   teaspoons canola oil

1 To make the salsa, stir together the pineapple, onion, cilantro, lime juice, ginger, jalapeño, and honey in a serving bowl.

2 Spray the broiler rack with nonstick spray and preheat the broiler.

3 Toss together the shrimp, jerk seasoning, and oil in a medium bowl until coated evenly. Thread about 7 shrimp on each of 4 (10- to 12-inch) metal skewers. Place the skewers on the broiler rack and broil 5 inches from the heat until the shrimp are just opaque in the center, about 3 minutes on each side. Serve with the salsa.

PER SERVING (1 skewer and 1/2 cup salsa): 157 Cal, 3 g Fat, 0 g Sat Fat, 0 g Trans Fat, 107 mg Chol, 136 mg Sod, 21 g Carb, 3 g Fib, 12 g Prot, 54 mg Calc. **POINTS** value: **3.**

## In the Kitchen

To keep the shrimp from turning on the skewers, thread each shrimp through 2 skewers placed about 3/4 inch apart. Serve a steaming bowl of fragrant jasmine rice alongside the shrimp (1/2 cup cooked jasmine rice for each serving will increase the **POINTS** value by **2**).

# Linguine with Cauliflower and Crushed Croutons

prep 20 min   cook 10 min   serves 4

8   ounces whole-wheat linguine

6   cups cauliflower florets

2   teaspoons olive oil

2   shallots, minced

2   garlic cloves, minced

1/4   teaspoon salt

1/4   teaspoon black pepper

1/2   cup multigrain croutons, coarsely crushed

1/4   cup chopped fresh parsley

3   tablespoons grated Romano cheese

1 Bring a large pot of water to a boil. Add the pasta and cook until almost al dente, about 5 minutes. Add the cauliflower to the pot and return the water to a boil. Cook, stirring occasionally, until the pasta and cauliflower are tender, about 3 minutes longer. Drain, reserving 1/4 cup of the cooking liquid.

2 Meanwhile, heat the oil in a large nonstick skillet over medium heat. Add the shallots and garlic; cook, stirring occasionally, until the shallots are softened, about 2 minutes. Add the pasta, cauliflower, salt, pepper, and the reserved cooking liquid; toss to coat evenly.

3 Transfer the pasta mixture to a serving bowl. Sprinkle with the croutons, parsley, and Romano.

PER SERVING (1³/4 cups): 310 Cal, 5 g Fat, 1 g Sat Fat, 0 g Trans Fat, 6 mg Chol, 497 mg Sod, 57 g Carb, 9 g Fib, 14 g Prot, 130 mg Calc. **POINTS** value: **6.**

## So Satisfying

Want to add a little heat to this classic combo of cauliflower and pasta? Add a generous pinch of red pepper flakes to the pasta mixture in step 2.

# Ziti with Spinach, Tomatoes, and White Beans

prep 10 min   cook 10 min   serves 4

8   ounces ziti or other tube pasta

1   tablespoon olive oil

3   large garlic cloves, minced

1   pound baby spinach

1   (15½-ounce) can small white beans, rinsed and drained

1   cup grape tomatoes

1   cup reduced-sodium chicken broth or water

¼   teaspoon salt

¼   teaspoon black pepper

¼   cup grated Parmesan cheese

1 Cook the pasta according to the package directions, omitting the salt if desired. Drain and keep warm.

2 Meanwhile, heat the oil in a large nonstick skillet over medium heat. Add the garlic and cook, stirring, until golden, about 1 minute. Add the spinach, a handful at a time, stirring until all the spinach is wilted, about 2 minutes.

3 Add the white beans, grape tomatoes, broth, salt, and pepper to the skillet; bring to a simmer over medium-high heat. Cook until the broth is slightly thickened, about 3 minutes. Stir in the pasta and cook, stirring, until heated through, about 1 minute longer. Serve sprinkled with the Parmesan.

PER SERVING (about 1¼ cups): 374 Cal, 8 g Fat, 2 g Sat Fat, 0 g Trans Fat, 7 mg Chol, 779 mg Sod, 60 g Carb, 11 g Fib, 16 g Prot, 189 mg Calc. **POINTS** value: **7.**

◆ Filling Extra
Add 2 cups sliced white or cremini mushrooms to the skillet along with the tomatoes in step 3.

# Caprese-Style Perciatelli

prep 15 min   cook 10 min   serves 4

½   pound perciatelli or spaghetti

2   cups grape tomatoes, halved

4   ounces bite-size bocconcini
     (small mozzarella balls)

¼   cup coarsely chopped fresh basil

2   garlic cloves, minced

½   teaspoon salt

½   teaspoon black pepper

3   tablespoons grated Grana
     Padano or Parmesan cheese

1 Prepare the pasta according to the package directions, omitting the salt if desired. Drain and keep warm.

2 Gently toss together all the remaining ingredients except the Grana Padano in a serving bowl. Add the pasta and cheese; toss to mix well.

PER SERVING (1 ¼ cups): 325 Cal, 9 g Fat, 5 g Sat Fat, 0 g Trans Fat, 44 mg Chol, 735 mg Sod, 48 g Carb, 6 g Fib, 24 g Prot, 305 mg Calc. **POINTS** value: **6.**

◆ Filling Extra

Add 1 cup of steamed diagonally cut green beans and/or some thickly sliced white mushrooms along with the pasta in step 2.

**CAPRESE-STYLE PERCIATELLI**

# Crisp 'n' Crunchy

chapter 2

# Oven-Roasted Chili Chickpeas

prep 5 min   roast 20 min   serves 4 as a light bite

1   **(15¹/₂-ounce) can chickpeas, rinsed, drained, and patted dry**

2   **teaspoons garlic salt**

1   **teaspoon chili powder**

1   **teaspoon grated lemon zest**

1 Preheat the oven to 450°F.

2 Spread the chickpeas in a jelly-roll pan. Roast the chickpeas, shaking the pan occasionally, until they begin to brown, about 20 minutes. Let cool about 5 minutes.

3 Lightly spray the chickpeas with olive oil nonstick spray. Sprinkle evenly with the garlic salt, chili powder, and lemon zest, shaking the pan to coat evenly. Transfer the chickpeas to a serving bowl.

PER SERVING (¹/₄ cup): 128 Cal, 2 g Fat, 0 g Sat Fat, 0 g Trans Fat, 0 mg Chol, 596 mg Sod, 22 g Carb, 5 g Fib, 7 g Prot, 43 mg Calc. **POINTS** value: **2.**

## So Satisfying

Crispy on the outside and tender on the inside, this garlicky, salty, chili-spiced snack will keep hunger pangs at bay any time of the day. Roast up a big batch, and store in a covered mason jar so it's right at hand. This recipe works with the Simply Filling technique.

# Garlicky Bean Dip with Sesame Wonton Crisps

prep 5 min   bake 5 min   serves 4 as a light bite

12   wonton wrappers

1   teaspoon sesame seeds

3/4   teaspoon salt

1   (15¹/₂-ounce) can cannellini (white kidney) beans, rinsed and drained

1   large garlic clove

1¹/₂ teaspoons finely chopped fresh rosemary

1¹/₂ teaspoons lemon juice

1¹/₂ teaspoons olive oil

¹/₂   teaspoon paprika

¹/₄   teaspoon black pepper

1 Preheat the oven to 375°F. Line a large baking sheet with parchment paper.

2 Stack the wonton wrappers and cut in half on a diagonal. Arrange the wontons, in one layer, on the prepared baking sheet. Lightly spray with nonstick spray; sprinkle with the sesame seeds and 1/4 teaspoon of the salt. Bake until golden and crispy, about 5 minutes.

3 Meanwhile, to make the dip, combine the beans, garlic, rosemary, lemon juice, oil, paprika, pepper, and the remaining 1/2 teaspoon salt in a food processor and puree. Transfer the dip to a serving bowl and serve with the wonton crisps.

PER SERVING (1/4 cup dip and 6 crisps): 204 Cal, 4 g Fat, 1 g Sat Fat, 0 g Trans Fat, 2 mg Chol, 688 mg Sod, 33 g Carb, 6 g Fib, 9 g Prot, 74 mg Calc. **POINTS** value: **4.**

◆ Filling Extra

Pick up some packaged baby-cut carrots, celery sticks, and jicama sticks—they're the perfect no-cook, no-fuss dippers for this boldly flavored bean dip.

# Grilled Prosciutto-Wrapped Asparagus

prep 5 min   grill 10 min   serves 4 as a light bite

1   **(1-pound) bunch asparagus, trimmed**

10  **very thin slices prosciutto (about 5 ounces), halved lengthwise**

1 Spray the grill rack with nonstick spray. Preheat the grill to medium-high or prepare a medium-high fire.

2 Tightly wrap a piece of prosciutto around each asparagus spear and lightly spray with olive oil nonstick spray. Place the wrapped spears on the grill rack and grill, turning, until the asparagus is tender and the prosciutto is crispy, about 10 minutes. Pile on a platter and serve hot, warm, or at room temperature.

PER SERVING (5 wrapped asparagus spears): 83 Cal, 5 g Fat, 2 g Sat Fat, 0 g Trans Fat, 18 mg Chol, 278 mg Sod, 2 g Carb, 1 g Fib, 7 g Prot, 17 mg Calc. **POINTS** value: **2.**

## So Satisfying

The prosciutto adds just enough tempting saltiness to flavor up the tender asparagus to a tee. If you like, grind some fresh black pepper over the stalks before wrapping them.

**FROM TOP CLOCKWISE: GARLICKY BEAN DIP WITH SESAME WONTON CRISPS, PAGE 53, OVEN-ROASTED CHILI CHICKPEAS, PAGE 52, AND GRILLED PROSCIUTTO-WRAPPED ASPARAGUS**

# Broiled Clams Oreganata

prep 15 min   broil 5 min   serves 4 as a light bite

1 cup fresh whole-wheat bread crumbs

1/2 cup finely chopped fresh parsley

2 garlic cloves, minced

1 tablespoon water

2 teaspoons olive oil

1/2 teaspoon dried oregano

1/4 teaspoon salt

1/4 teaspoon black pepper

2 dozen littleneck clams, shucked, bottom shells reserved

1 lemon, cut into wedges

1 Preheat the broiler. Line the broiler rack with foil.

2 Stir together the bread crumbs, parsley, garlic, water, oil, oregano, salt, and pepper in a small bowl until the crumbs are evenly moistened. Stir in a little additional water, if needed.

3 Place each clam in a half shell and top with a heaping teaspoon of the bread crumb mixture. Place the clams on the broiler rack and broil 5 inches from the heat until the clams are cooked through and the topping is golden brown and crispy, about 5 minutes. Serve with the lemon wedges.

PER SERVING (6 clams): 186 Cal, 4 g Fat, 1 g Sat Fat, 0 g Trans Fat, 40 mg Chol, 243 mg Sod, 20 g Carb, 3 g Fib, 19 g Prot, 82 mg Calc. **POINTS** value: **3.**

## In the Kitchen

You will need about 2 slices of whole-wheat bread to make 1 cup of crumbs. Tear the bread into pieces, toss into your food processor, and process until crumbs form.

# Endive-Apple Salad with Sherry Vinegar Dressing

prep 10 min   cook none   serves 4

| | |
|---|---|
| 2 | Belgian endive, leaves separated |
| 1 | red apple, halved, cored, and cut into thin wedges |
| 2 | tablespoons walnuts, toasted and chopped |
| 3 | tablespoons warm water |
| 1 | tablespoon sherry vinegar |
| 2 | teaspoons olive oil |
| 2 | teaspoons Dijon mustard |
| 1/2 | teaspoon salt |
| 1/4 | teaspoon black pepper |
| 1/4 | cup crumbled reduced-fat feta cheese |

1 Toss together the endive, apple, and walnuts in a serving bowl.

2 To make the dressing, whisk together all the remaining ingredients except the feta in a small bowl until blended. Drizzle the dressing over the salad and toss to coat evenly. Divide the salad evenly among 4 plates and sprinkle with the feta.

PER SERVING (about 1 1/4 cups): 98 Cal, 5 g Fat, 1 g Sat Fat, 0 g Trans Fat, 3 mg Chol, 479 mg Sod, 11 g Carb, 3 g Fib, 3 g Prot, 74 mg Calc. *POINTS* value: 2.

◆ Filling Extra

Use 3 endive instead of 2 and toss in some torn frisée. The salad will look—and taste—even more fabulous.

**SHRIMP AND MANGO SUMMER ROLLS**

# Shrimp and Mango Summer Rolls

prep 20 minutes   cook none   serves 4

2   tablespoons unseasoned rice vinegar

2   tablespoons fish sauce

2   tablespoons lime juice

2   tablespoons hoisin sauce

2   tablespoons minced peeled fresh ginger

1   tablespoon + 1 teaspoon Sriracha (hot chili sauce)

8   (8-inch) rice-paper rounds

1/2   pound cooked medium shrimp

2   cups packaged coleslaw mix (from a 10-ounce package)

1   mango, peeled and cut into thick matchsticks

1/4   cup chopped fresh cilantro

1/4   cup chopped fresh mint

Lime wedges

1 To make the dipping sauce, whisk together the rice vinegar, fish sauce, lime juice, hoisin sauce, ginger, and Sriracha in a serving bowl.

2 Soak the rice-paper rounds, one at a time, in a large bowl of hot water just until softened, 10–30 seconds. Place the rice-paper rounds, as they are softened, on a double layer of paper towels to drain.

3 Lay the softened wrappers out on a work surface. Arrange about 5 shrimp along the center of each wrapper leaving a border at the top and bottom; layer evenly with the coleslaw mix, mango, cilantro, and mint. Fold in the sides of the wrappers and roll up tightly to enclose the filling. Cut each roll in half on a diagonal and serve with the dipping sauce.

PER SERVING (2 summer rolls and about 2 tablespoons sauce): 204 Cal, 2 g Fat, 0 g Sat Fat, 0 g Trans Fat, 47 mg Chol, 1054 mg Sod, 40 g Carb, 4 g Fib, 8 g Prot, 52 mg Calc. *POINTS* value: *3.*

## In the Kitchen

Summer rolls, also called spring rolls, are a popular Vietnamese snack. They typically consist of cooked shrimp or pork layered with crunchy vegetables, cooked rice noodles and fresh mint and cilantro leaves. Unlike Chinese spring rolls, which are fried, summer rolls are simply wrapped in rice-paper rounds.

# Fennel-Orange Salad with Cracked Pepper and Mint

prep 10 min   cook none   serves 4

1   large fennel bulb

1   large orange, peeled and sectioned

6   large brine-cured black olives, pitted and chopped

1/2   cup coarsely chopped fresh mint

2   tablespoons orange juice

2   teaspoons balsamic vinegar

2   teaspoons walnut oil

1   teaspoon olive oil

1/2   teaspoon cracked black pepper

1 Cut the fennel lengthwise in half and thinly slice. Reserve the feathery fonds.

2 Toss together the fennel, orange, olives, and mint in a large bowl.

3 To make the dressing, whisk together the remaining ingredients in a small bowl until blended. Drizzle the dressing over the salad and toss to coat. Divide the salad evenly among 4 plates. Chop enough of the reserved fennel fronds to equal 1/4 cup. Sprinkle evenly over the salads.

PER SERVING (1 cup): 88 Cal, 4 g Fat, 0 g Sat Fat, 0 g Trans Fat, 0 mg Chol, 93 mg Sod, 12 g Carb, 4 g Fib, 2 g Prot, 67 mg Calc. **POINTS** value: **1.**

## In the Kitchen
A vegetable slicer, also known as a V-slicer, makes quick and easy work of producing paper-thin slices of fennel.

# Iceberg Wedges with Creamy Blue Cheese Dressing

prep 10 min  cook 5 min  serves 4

1/3  cup low-fat buttermilk

1/3  cup fat-free sour cream

1/4  cup crumbled blue cheese

2    tablespoons lemon juice

1/4  teaspoon black pepper

1    small head iceberg lettuce

1    cup cherry tomatoes, halved

12   tender watercress sprigs

2    slices turkey bacon, crisp cooked and crumbled

1 Combine the buttermilk, sour cream, blue cheese, lemon juice, and pepper in a blender and puree.

2 Cut the lettuce into 4 equal wedges and place 1 wedge, cut side down, on each of 4 plates. Scatter the tomatoes around the lettuce and top each wedge with 3 watercress sprigs. Drizzle the dressing over the lettuce and tomatoes and top evenly with the bacon.

PER SERVING (1 lettuce wedge, 1/4 cup tomatoes, 3 watercress sprigs, 1/2 slice bacon, and about 1/4 cup dressing): 102 Cal, 5 g Fat, 2 g Sat Fat, 0 g Trans Fat, 16 mg Chol, 342 mg Sod, 9 g Carb, 2 g Fib, 7 g Prot, 123 mg Calc. **POINTS** value: **2.**

◆ Filling Extra
Add a peppery bite to this salad by topping the watercress with thinly sliced radishes.

# Chopped Salad with Russian Dressing

prep 20 min   cook none   serves 4

¹/₂  cup fat-free mayonnaise

¹/₂  cup low-fat buttermilk

¹/₄  cup sweet pickle relish

¹/₄  cup ketchup

1    tablespoon hot pepper sauce
     (such as Frank's)

2    celery stalks, cut into ³/₈-inch
     dice

2    large carrots, cut into ³/₈-inch
     dice

1    large cucumber, peeled, halved,
     seeded, and cut into ³/₈-inch dice

1    large tomato, seeded and cut
     into ³/₈-inch dice

1    small yellow or red bell pepper,
     cut into ³/₈-inch dice

1    sweet onion, cut into ³/₈-inch
     dice

¹/₄  cup (¹/₂-inch) diced reduced-fat
     sharp cheddar cheese

1 To make the dressing, whisk together the mayonnaise, buttermilk, relish, ketchup, and hot sauce in a small bowl.

2 Combine the remaining ingredients in a serving bowl and gently toss to mix. Drizzle with the dressing and toss to coat evenly.

PER SERVING (about 1¹/₄ cups): 132 Cal, 2 g Fat, 1 g Sat Fat, 0 g Trans Fat, 6 mg Chol, 770 mg Sod, 26 g Carb, 4 g Fib, 5 g Prot, 134 mg Calc. *POINTS* value: *2.*

◆ Filling Extra

Turn this salad into a satisfying lunch or light supper dish by adding diced chicken breast (3 ounces diced cooked chicken breast for each serving will increase the *POINTS* value by *3*).

# Fennel-Carrot Slaw with Orange–Poppy Seed Dressing

prep 15 min   cook none   serves 4

1/3   cup light sour cream

1/2   teaspoon grated orange zest

3   tablespoons orange juice

2   teaspoons honey

2   teaspoons poppy seeds

1/2   teaspoon salt

1/4   teaspoon black pepper

1   large fennel bulb, halved lengthwise and cut into matchsticks

1   jicama or large Granny Smith apple, peeled and cut into matchsticks (about 2 cups)

2   cups packaged matchstick-cut carrots

6   large radishes, thinly sliced, (about 1 cup)

1 To make the dressing, whisk together the sour cream, orange zest and juice, honey, poppy seeds, salt, and pepper in a small bowl.

2 Toss together the remaining ingredients in a serving bowl. Add the dressing and toss to coat evenly. Serve or cover and refrigerate up to 4 hours.

PER SERVING (about 1 1/4 cups): 111 Cal, 2 g Fat, 1 g Sat Fat, 0 g Trans Fat, 7 mg Chol, 400 mg Sod, 21 g Carb, 6 g Fib, 3 g Prot, 110 mg Calc. **POINTS** value: **2.**

## In the Kitchen

Jicama is a large rock-shaped root vegetable. Once all of its brown, fibrous skin is peeled away, pristine white, firm flesh is revealed. Jicama is often thought of as a cross between a white potato and a Granny Smith apple and has the crunchy texture of a radish. Best of all, it is equally delicious raw and cooked.

# Sweet 'n' Sour Caribbean Slaw

prep 15 min   cook none   serves 4

1½ cups shredded red cabbage (from a 10-ounce package)

1½ cups coleslaw mix (from a 16-ounce package)

½ cup packaged matchstick-cut carrots

½ red bell pepper, thinly sliced

½ small sweet onion, thinly sliced

2 tablespoons light sour cream

2 tablespoons fat-free half-and-half

2 tablespoons white vinegar

2 tablespoons packed brown sugar

½ teaspoon salt

1 teaspoon sesame seeds, preferably toasted

1 Combine the cabbage, coleslaw mix, carrots, bell pepper, and onion and in a serving bowl.

2 To make the dressing, whisk together the sour cream, half-and-half, vinegar, brown sugar, and salt in a small bowl. Add the mayonnaise mixture to the cabbage mixture and toss to coat evenly. Sprinkle with the sesame seeds. Serve or cover and refrigerate up to 4 hours. Toss again just before serving.

PER SERVING (1 cup): 75 Cal, 2 g Fat, 1 g Sat Fat, 0 g Trans Fat, 3 mg Chol, 334 mg Sod, 14 g Carb, 2 g Fib, 2 g Prot, 52 mg Calc. **POINTS** value: **1.**

## ◆ Filling Extra

Make this very tasty side dish more filling and more nutritious by adding a 15½-ounce can of black beans, rinsed and drained, to the cabbage mixture in step 1. The **POINTS** value for each serving will increase by **1.**

**SWEET 'N' SOUR CARIBBEAN SLAW**

# Pan-Roasted Asparagus with Fried Capers

prep 5 min   cook 5 min   serves 4

1    (1-pound) bunch asparagus, trimmed

2    teaspoons olive oil

2    tablespoons capers, drained and patted dry

1    tablespoon pine nuts, toasted

1/2   lemon, thinly sliced

1 Spray a large nonstick skillet with nonstick spray and set over medium-high heat. Add the asparagus and cook, shaking the pan occasionally, until crisp-tender, about 5 minutes.

2 Heat the oil in a small skillet over medium-high heat. Add the capers and cook, stirring, until crispy, about 2 minutes.

3 Arrange the asparagus on a platter and sprinkle with the capers and pine nuts. Garnish with the lemon slices.

PER SERVING (about 5 garnished asparagus): 49 Cal, 4 g Fat, 0 g Sat Fat, 0 g Trans Fat, 0 mg Chol, 129 mg Sod, 3 g Carb, 2 g Fib, 2 g Prot, 18 mg Calc. **POINTS** value: **1.**

◆ Filling Extra
Add a good handful (about 1 cup) of halved grape or cherry tomatoes to the skillet after the asparagus has cooked for 3 minutes.

# Light-as-a-Feather Corn Fritters

prep 15 min   cook 10 min   serves 4

¹/₄  cup all-purpose flour

¹/₂  teaspoon ground cumin

¹/₂  teaspoon salt

¹/₄  teaspoon baking powder

¹/₄  teaspoon black pepper

¹/₂  cup low-fat buttermilk

1    large egg

1    (14-ounce) package frozen shoe peg (baby white and yellow) corn kernels, thawed

3    large egg whites

1    tablespoon olive oil

Pure maple syrup (optional)

1 Whisk together the flour, cumin, salt, baking powder, and pepper in a large bowl. Whisk together the buttermilk and egg in a small bowl until blended. Add the buttermilk mixture to the flour mixture and stir until combined; stir in the corn.

2 With an electric mixer on medium-high speed or with a clean whisk, beat the egg whites just until stiff peaks form. Fold the whites into the batter just until blended.

3 Heat 1¹/₂ teaspoons of the oil in a large nonstick skillet over medium-high heat. Drop 12 heaping teaspoonfuls of the batter into the skillet and cook until browned, about 2 minutes on each side. Repeat with the remaining oil and batter to make a total of 24 fritters, spraying the skillet with nonstick spray between batches if needed. Serve with maple syrup if using.

PER SERVING (6 fritters without maple syrup): 181 Cal, 6 g Fat, 1 g Sat Fat, 0 g Trans Fat, 54 mg Chol, 416 mg Sod, 26 g Carb, 3 g Fib, 9 g Prot, 68 mg Calc. *POINTS* value: *4.*

## In the Kitchen

These fritters are sure to be the lightest ones you've ever had, thanks to the small amount of flour and the lightening effect of beaten egg whites. For a little variety, substitute an equal amount shredded zucchini (squeezed dry of excess moisture) for the corn, and toss in a pinch of cayenne for a little oomph.

# Ultimate Onion Rings

prep 10 min   bake 20 min   serves 4

¹/₃  cup all-purpose flour

1    cup low-fat buttermilk

¹/₂  teaspoon salt

¹/₂  teaspoon black pepper

¹/₂  cup plain dried bread crumbs

¹/₂  teaspoon Old Bay Seasoning

2    large sweet onions, cut crosswise into ¹/₂-inch rounds and separated into 32 rings

1 Preheat the oven to 450°F. Spray two large baking sheets with nonstick spray.

2 Put the flour in a large zip-close plastic bag. Whisk together the buttermilk, salt, and pepper in a shallow bowl. Combine the bread crumbs and Old Bay seasoning in a large shallow bowl.

3 Add the onion rings, a few at a time, to the flour and shake to coat. Dip the rings, one at a time, in the buttermilk mixture, then coat with the bread crumbs, transferring the rings as they are coated to the prepared baking sheets. Bake until golden and crispy, about 20 minutes.

PER SERVING (8 onion rings): 147 Cal, 1 g Fat, 1 g Sat Fat, 0 g Trans Fat, 2 mg Chol, 541 mg Sod, 28 g Carb, 3 g Fib, 6 g Prot, 117 mg Calc. **POINTS** value: **2.**

## In the Kitchen

It is the high oven temperature that gives these flavorful onion rings their extra crispiness. Use an oven thermometer to check the accuracy of your oven.

# Parmesan and Cornmeal–Crusted Fried Tomatoes

prep 5 min    cook 10 min    serves 4

½   cup cornmeal

½   cup grated Parmesan cheese

1    teaspoon dried oregano

½   teaspoon salt

½   teaspoon black pepper

3    very firm large red or green
      tomatoes, cut into ½-inch slices

1 Mix together the cornmeal, Parmesan, oregano, salt, and pepper in a small bowl. Coat the tomato slices, one at a time, in the cornmeal mixture.

2 Spray a large heavy skillet with nonstick spray and set over medium-high heat. Add the tomatoes, in batches, and cook until golden brown, about 4 minutes on each side, spraying the skillet with nonstick spray between batches.

PER SERVING (about 3 tomato slices): 160 Cal, 5 g Fat, 2 g Sat Fat, 0 g Trans Fat, 10 mg Chol, 529 mg Sod, 22 g Carb, 3 g Fib, 8 g Prot, 187 mg Calc. **POINTS** value: **3.**

## In The Kitchen

The secret to achieving a golden brown crust with a minimum of oil is using a heavy-bottomed skillet that is screamingly hot when the tomatoes are added. If you own a cast-iron skillet, be sure to use it here.

**CUMIN-SCENTED SWEET POTATO WEDGES AND ULTIMATE ONION RINGS, PAGE 68**

# Cumin-Scented Sweet Potato Wedges

prep 5 min   grill 15 min   serves 4

**2**    large sweet potatoes (10 ounces each), peeled, each cut into 8 wedges

**1**    teaspoon ground cumin

**1**    teaspoon paprika

**³/₄**   teaspoon salt

**¹/₂**   teaspoon black pepper

1 Spray the grill rack with nonstick spray. Preheat the grill to high or prepare a hot fire.

2 Put the sweet potato wedges in a large bowl and spray with olive oil nonstick spray; toss to coat evenly. Combine the remaining ingredients in a cup; sprinkle evenly over the potatoes. Toss to coat.

3 Arrange the potatoes, cut side down, on the grill rack and grill until tender and crispy in spots, about 7 minutes on each cut side.

PER SERVING (4 potato wedges): 95 Cal, 1 g Fat, 0 g Sat Fat, 0 g Trans Fat, 0 mg Chol, 476 mg Sod, 19 g Carb, 3 g Fib, 2 g Prot, 41 mg Calc. **POINTS** value: **1.**

## So Satisfying
When nothing but thick potato wedges will do, this is the recipe to turn to. Crispy and spicy on the outside and moist and tender on the inside, these are hard to beat. For variety, substitute a large baking potato for one of the sweet potatoes. This recipe works with the Simply Filling technique.

# Pepper and Coriander–Crusted Filet Mignon with Wild Mushrooms

prep 15 min   cook/grill 10 min   serves 4

| | |
|---|---|
| 2 | tablespoons whole black peppercorns |
| 2 | tablespoons coriander seeds |
| 1/2 | teaspoon salt |
| 1 | (1-pound) beef tenderloin, trimmed |
| 2 | teaspoons olive oil |
| 1 | small onion, chopped |
| 1 | pound mixed wild mushrooms, sliced |
| 2 | tablespoons fresh thyme leaves |
| 3 | tablespoons dry white wine or dry vermouth |

1 Spray the grill rack with nonstick spray. Preheat the grill to medium-high or prepare a medium-high fire.

2 Combine the peppercorns, coriander seeds, and salt in a small zip-close plastic bag. With a meat mallet or the bottom of a heavy saucepan, crush the mixture. Spread the peppercorn mixture on a sheet of wax paper. Roll the tenderloin in the peppercorn mixture to coat evenly, pressing it into the meat so it adheres. Cut the beef into 4 equal-size filets mignons.

3 Heat the oil in a large nonstick skillet over medium-high heat. Add the onion and cook, stirring, until softened, about 5 minutes. Add the mushrooms and thyme; cook, stirring, until the mushrooms are browned, about 5 minutes. Add the wine and cook, stirring, until the mushrooms are tender, about 2 minutes longer. Remove the skillet from the heat and keep warm.

4 Meanwhile, place the filets on the grill rack and grill until an instant-read thermometer inserted into the side of a steak registers 145°F for medium-rare, about 5 minutes on each side. Serve with the mushrooms.

PER SERVING (1 filet mignon and about 1/2 cup mushrooms): 235 Cal, 10 g Fat, 3 g Sat Fat, 0 g Trans Fat, 42 mg Chol, 342 mg Sod, 12 g Carb, 4 g Fib, 27 g Prot, 59 mg Calc. *POINTS* value: **5.**

◆ Filling Extra
Serve with a bowl of steamed green beans drizzled with lemon juice and seasoned with salt and pepper.

# Crispy Thai Beef Salad with Ginger-Lime Dressing

prep 15 min   cook 10 min   serves 4

¹/₄  cup lime juice

2   tablespoons fish sauce

2   teaspoons packed brown sugar

2   teaspoons grated peeled
    fresh ginger

1   teaspoon Sriracha (hot chili
    sauce)

1   pound round steak, trimmed
    and thinly sliced

3   cups thinly sliced Napa cabbage

1   small red onion, thinly sliced

¹/₃  cup packaged matchstick-cut
    carrots

¹/₂  cup chopped fresh mint

¹/₄  cup chopped fresh cilantro

¹/₄  cup unsalted dry-roasted
    peanuts, finely chopped

1 To make the dressing, whisk together the lime juice, fish sauce, brown sugar, ginger, and Sriracha in a small bowl.

2 Put the beef in a large bowl and drizzle with 1 tablespoon of the dressing; toss until coated evenly. Spray a nonstick grill pan or large nonstick skillet with nonstick spray and set over medium-high heat. Place some of the slices of beef on the grill pan and cook, turning occasionally, until browned and crispy along the edges, about 10 minutes. Repeat with the remaining beef, transferring it to a large plate.

3 Layer the cabbage, onion, carrots, and mint on a platter; top with the steak and sprinkle with the cilantro and peanuts. Drizzle with the remaining dressing.

PER SERVING (1¹/₄ cups): 282 Cal, 9 g Fat, 2 g Sat Fat, 0 g Trans Fat, 84 mg Chol, 827 mg Sod, 12 g Carb, 3 g Fib, 38 g Prot, 90 mg Calc. **POINTS** value: **6.**

◆ Filling Extra

A bowl of brown basmati rice turns the salad into heartier fare (¹/₂ cup cooked brown basmati rice for each serving will increase the **POINTS** value by **2**).

# Beef Sliders with Slaw

prep 10 min   grill 10 min   serves 4

¼   cup low-fat mayonnaise

1½ teaspoons cider vinegar

1   teaspoon celery seeds

1   (10-ounce) bag broccoli slaw

1   pound ground lean beef (7% fat or less)

½   teaspoon salt

¼   teaspoon black pepper

16   (3-inch round or square) slices crusty whole-grain bread

1 Spray the grill rack with nonstick spray. Preheat the grill to high or prepare a hot fire.

2 To make the slaw, whisk together the mayonnaise, vinegar, and celery seeds in a medium bowl. Add the broccoli slaw and toss to coat.

3 With damp hands, shape the beef into 8 (½-inch-thick) patties. Sprinkle with the salt and pepper. Spray the bread on both sides with olive oil nonstick spray.

4 Place the patties on the grill rack and grill until an instant-read thermometer inserted into the side of a burger registers 160°F for well done, about 5 minutes on each side. After the burgers have cooked for 4 minutes, put the bread on the grill rack and grill until browned and crispy, about 3 minutes on each side. Place a burger on each of 8 slices of bread and top evenly with the slaw. Cover with the remaining slices of bread.

PER SERVING (2 sliders): 371 Cal, 14 g Fat, 4 g Sat Fat, 0 g Trans Fat, 69 mg Chol, 739 mg Sod, 30 g Carb, 6 g Fib, 32 g Prot, 113 mg Calc. **POINTS** value: **8.**

## In the Kitchen

In case you haven't heard, sliders (mini burgers served on mini buns) are all the rage in restaurants these days. They are small enough so that a serving is usually two or three of them. Their popularity is probably due to the fact that they are simply more fun to eat than a large burger.

**BEEF SLIDERS WITH SLAW**

# Pressed Cuban Sandwiches

prep 5 min   cook 5 min   serves 2

| | |
|---|---|
| 1 | tablespoon yellow mustard |
| 2 | (2½-ounce) whole-grain rolls, split |
| 2 | (1-ounce) slices fat-free deli turkey |
| 2 | (1-ounce) slices lean low-sodium deli ham |
| 2 | (1-ounce) slices reduced-fat Swiss cheese |
| 6 | thin slices dill pickle |

1 Preheat a large cast-iron or other heavy skillet over medium-high heat or preheat a panini press to high.

2 Spread the mustard over the bottom half of each roll; layer evenly with the turkey, ham, Swiss cheese, and pickle. Cover with the tops of the rolls.

3 Place the sandwiches in the skillet and top with another heavy skillet to weight them. Cook until the cheese is melted and the bread is golden brown and crispy, about 2 minutes on each side (or grill the sandwiches in the panini press).

PER SERVING (1 sandwich): 305 Cal, 6 g Fat, 3 g Sat Fat, 0 g Trans Fat, 39 mg Chol, 1175 mg Sod, 33 g Carb, 6 g Fib, 29 g Prot, 371 mg Calc. **POINTS** value: **6.**

## So Satisfying

The key to a great Cuban sandwich is the bread. It needs to be super-crispy on the outside and moist and tender on the inside. Serve these sandwiches with a side of thinly sliced red or green cabbage slaw dressed with some fresh lemon juice, canola oil, salt, and pepper.

# Parmesan and Panko–Crusted Lamb Chops

prep 10   cook 5 min   serves 4

2   tablespoons Dijon mustard

1   large garlic clove, minced

2   teaspoons minced fresh
    rosemary

1   teaspoon salt

1/4   teaspoon black pepper

8   (3-ounce) lamb rib chops,
    trimmed

1/4   cup grated Parmesan cheese

1/4   cup whole-wheat panko
    (Japanese bread crumbs)

1 Stir together the mustard, garlic, rosemary, salt, and pepper in a cup. Spread evenly on one side of each lamb chop.

2 Combine the Parmesan and panko on a small plate. Press the mustard-coated side of each chop into the Parmesan mixture, pressing lightly so it adheres.

3 Spray a large nonstick skillet with nonstick spray and set over medium-high heat. Add the chops, Parmesan side down, and cook until crusty and browned, about 3 minutes. Spray the chops with nonstick spray. Turn and cook until an instant-read thermometer inserted into the side of a chop registers 145°F for medium-rare, about 3 minutes longer.

PER SERVING (2 lamb chops): 187 Cal, 10 g Fat, 4 g Sat Fat, 0 g Trans Fat, 55 mg Chol, 942 mg Sod, 5 g Carb, 1 g Fib, 19 g Prot, 105 mg Calc. **POINTS** value: **4.**

## In the Kitchen

Whole-wheat panko is available in specialty-foods stores and in organic-foods supermarkets.

# Pork and Tomato Carnitas

prep 10 min   cook 20 min   serves 4

| | |
|---|---|
| 2 | teaspoons canola oil |
| 1 | pound pork tenderloin, cut into 2-inch strips |
| 1 | white onion, thinly sliced |
| 2 | large garlic cloves, minced |
| 1 | (14$^1$/$_2$-ounce) can diced tomatoes |
| 1 | tablespoon red-wine vinegar |
| 2 | teaspoons ancho or regular chili powder |
| 1 | teaspoon ground cumin |
| $^1$/$_2$ | teaspoon salt |
| $^1$/$_4$ | cup chopped fresh cilantro |
| 8 | (6-inch) corn tortillas, warmed |

1 Heat the oil in a large nonstick skillet over medium-high heat. Add the pork, onion, and garlic; cook, stirring, until the pork and onion begin to brown, about 10 minutes. Stir in the tomatoes, vinegar, chile powder, cumin, and salt. Reduce the heat and simmer, stirring occasionally, about 10 minutes. Stir in the cilantro.

2 Meanwhile, heat a medium skillet over medium-high heat. Add the tortillas, one at a time, and cook until crispy and browned in spots, about 2 minutes. Turn and crisp on the second side, about 2 minutes longer.

3 Lay the warm tortillas out on a work surface and spoon 3/4 cup of the pork mixture along the middle of each tortilla; fold in half to enclose the filling.

PER SERVING (2 carnitas): 290 Cal, 9 g Fat, 2 g Sat Fat, 0 g Trans Fat, 48 mg Chol, 526 mg Sod, 29 g Carb, 5 g Fib, 26 g Prot, 93 mg Calc. **POINTS** value: **6.**

◈ Filling Extra

Turn our carnitas into bean tostadas by stirring a 15$^1$/$_2$-ounce can of black beans, rinsed and drained, into the pork mixture and heating through. Top the tortillas with sliced romaine lettuce and the pork mixture, then sprinkle with chopped tomato and onion. The **POINTS** value for each serving will increase by **1.**

**PORK AND TOMATO CARNITAS**

# Cayenne-Spiked Oven-Fried Chicken

prep 5 min   bake 25 min   serves 4

¼   cup whole-wheat panko
     (Japanese bread crumbs)

2   tablespoons all-purpose flour

1   teaspoon dried rosemary

1   teaspoon dried sage

1   teaspoon salt

½   teaspoon black pepper

½   teaspoon cayenne

¾   cup low-fat buttermilk

8   (3½-ounce) chicken drumsticks,
     skin removed

1 Preheat the oven to 450°F. Line the broiler pan with foil.

2 Mix together the panko, flour, rosemary, sage, salt, pepper, and cayenne in a large shallow bowl. Pour the buttermilk into another bowl. Dip the drumsticks, one at a time, into the buttermilk mixture, then roll in the panko mixture to coat evenly.

3 Spray the chicken with nonstick spray and place in the broiler pan. Bake until crispy and cooked through, about 25 minutes.

PER SERVING (2 drumsticks): 175 Cal, 4 g Fat, 1 g Sat Fat, 0 g Trans Fat, 87 mg Chol, 704 mg Sod, 9 g Carb, 1 g Fib, 25 g Prot, 82 mg Calc. **POINTS** value: **4.**

◆ Filling Extra
Turn this delicious spiced-up chicken into a complete meal by serving it with corn on the cob and thick slices of juicy tomato (1 medium ear of corn for each serving will increase the **POINTS** value by **1**).

# Summertime Chicken Panzanella Salad

prep 20 min   cook none   serves 4

12   ounces day-old crusty whole-grain bread, lightly toasted and cut into 1-inch chunks

$^1/_2$   pound cooked skinless boneless chicken breast, cut into bite-size pieces

2   large tomatoes, cut into $^3/_4$-inch chunks

1   red or yellow bell pepper, cut into $^3/_4$-inch chunks

$^1/_2$   seedless (English) cucumber, quartered lengthwise and cut into $^3/_4$-inch slices

1   small red onion, thinly sliced

$^1/_2$   cup chopped fresh flat-leaf parsley

10   fresh basil leaves, thinly sliced

2   tablespoons capers, rinsed and drained

$^1/_2$   cup fat-free Italian dressing

$^1/_2$   teaspoon black pepper

$^1/_4$   teaspoon salt

Combine the bread, chicken, tomatoes, bell pepper, cucumber, onion, parsley, basil, and capers in a serving bowl; toss well to mix. Drizzle with the dressing and sprinkle with the black pepper and salt; toss to coat.

PER SERVING (2 cups): 367 Cal, 6 g Fat, 2 g Sat Fat, 0 g Trans Fat, 49 mg Chol, 1152 mg Sod, 47 g Carb, 9 g Fib, 31 g Prot, 148 mg Calc. **POINTS** value: **7.**

## In the Kitchen

Here's how we quickly and easily slice fresh basil leaves. Stack the slices, roll them up lengthwise, and thinly slice. Easy and done!

**GOLDEN PHYLLO-TOPPED TURKEY POTPIE**

# Golden Phyllo–Topped Turkey Potpie

prep 10 min   cook/bake 25 min   serves 4

1   (8-ounce) package white or cremini mushrooms, thinly sliced

1/2   pound deli roast turkey breast, cut into 1/2-inch pieces

1   (16-ounce) package frozen corn kernels, thawed

1   (16-ounce) package frozen lima beans, thawed

1   tablespoon all-purpose flour

2   teaspoons dry mustard

1   teaspoon dried thyme

1/2   cup reduced-sodium chicken broth

2   tablespoons fat-free half-and-half

1   teaspoon Dijon mustard

1   teaspoon black pepper

1/4   teaspoon salt

4   (12 x 17-inch) sheets frozen phyllo dough, thawed

1 Preheat the oven to 350°F.

2 Spray a large nonstick skillet with nonstick spray and set over medium-high heat. Add the mushrooms and cook until softened, about 5 minutes. Stir in the turkey, corn, and lima beans. Sprinkle the flour, dry mustard, and thyme over the mushroom mixture and cook, stirring, 1 minute. Stir in the broth, half-and-half, Dijon mustard, pepper, and salt; bring to a boil. Reduce the heat and simmer, stirring occasionally, until the sauce bubbles and thickens, about 5 minutes.

3 Transfer the turkey mixture to a 2-quart baking dish. Lightly spray 1 sheet of phyllo with nonstick spray and crumple into a very loose ball; place on top of the filling. Repeat with the remaining phyllo to cover the filling. Bake until the phyllo is golden brown and crisp, about 15 minutes.

PER SERVING (1/4 of potpie): 358 Cal, 4 g Fat, 1 g Sat Fat, 0 g Trans Fat, 28 mg Chol, 1123 mg Sod, 61 g Carb, 10 g Fib, 24 g Prot, 68 mg Calc. *POINTS* value: *7.*

# Horseradish and Panko–Crusted Salmon

prep 5 min   bake/broil 15 min   serves 4

**4** **(6-ounce) skinless salmon filets**

**¹/₂** **teaspoon salt**

**¹/₄** **teaspoon black pepper**

**¹/₄** **cup beet horseradish, well drained**

**¹/₂** **cup whole-wheat panko (Japanese bread crumbs)**

**Lemon wedges**

1 Place an oven rack in the upper third of the oven and preheat the oven to 425°F. Line the broiler rack with foil.

2 Place the salmon, skinned side down, on the broiler rack and sprinkle with the salt and pepper. Top evenly with the horseradish, then with the panko, lightly pressing down. Lightly spray the panko with nonstick spray. Bake until the salmon is just opaque in the center, about 12 minutes.

3 Preheat the broiler. Broil the fish 5 inches from the heat until the panko is deep golden brown, about 3 minutes. Serve with lemon wedges.

PER SERVING (1 salmon fillet): 289 Cal, 11 g Fat, 3 g Sat Fat, 0 g Trans Fat, 111 mg Chol, 454 mg Sod, 10 g Carb, 2 g Fib, 38 g Prot, 34 mg Calc. **POINTS** value: **6**.

◆ Filling Extra

Turn this salmon dish into a complete meal by serving it with steamed sugar snap peas and wild rice (¹/₂ cup cooked wild rice for each serving will increase the **POINTS** value by **2**).

# Potato Chip–Coated Sea Bass

prep 5 min   bake 15 min   serves 4

2   tablespoons fat-free mayonnaise

1   tablespoon barbecue sauce

4   (6-ounce) sea bass fillets

2   cups baked barbecue flavor
    potato chips

1 Place an oven rack in the upper third of the oven and preheat the oven to 425°F. Line the broiler rack with foil.

2 Stir together the mayonnaise and barbecue sauce in a cup.

3 Place the bass fillets, skin side down, on the broiler rack; spread the mayonnaise mixture evenly over the tops of the fillets.

4 Place the potato chips in a large zip-close plastic bag. With a rolling pin or a meat mallet, coarsely crush the chips. Top the fish evenly with the chips and lightly spray with nonstick spray. Bake until the fish is just opaque in the center, about 12 minutes.

5 Preheat the broiler. Broil the fish 5 inches from the heat until the potato chip topping is lightly browned, about 30 seconds.

PER SERVING (1 bass fillet): 234 Cal, 4 g Fat, 1 g Sat Fat, 0 g Trans Fat, 92 mg Chol, 346 mg Sod, 14 g Carb, 1 g Fib, 33 g Prot, 31 mg Calc. *POINTS* value: **5.**

◆ Filling Extra
Serve the fish with bowls of steamed broccoli florets and cooked quinoa (1/2 cup cooked quinoa for each serving will increase the *POINTS* value by **2**).

# Jalapeño and Cilantro–Flavored Codfish Cakes

prep 15 min   cook 10 min   serves 4

| | |
|---|---|
| 1 | **pound cod fillets, skin removed** |
| 1 | **small onion, grated** |
| 1 | **large garlic clove, minced** |
| 1 | **small jalapeño pepper, seeded and minced** |
| 1/4 | **cup chopped fresh cilantro** |
| 1 | **tablespoon lime juice** |
| 1 | **teaspoon salt** |
| 1/4 | **cup + 2 tablespoons plain dried bread crumbs** |
| 2 | **large eggs, lightly beaten** |
| | **Lime Wedges** |

1 Using a large knife or a food processor, chop the cod. Mix together the cod, onion, garlic, jalapeño, cilantro, lime juice, and salt in a large bowl. Add 1/4 cup of the bread crumbs and the eggs, stirring until mixed.

2 With damp hands, shape the cod mixture into 12 (1/2-inch-thick) patties. Sprinkle the patties on both sides with the remaining 2 tablespoons bread crumbs.

3 Spray a large nonstick skillet with nonstick spray and set over medium-high heat. Add the patties to the skillet and cook until cooked throughout and crispy, about 5 minutes on each side. Pile the codfish cakes on a platter. Serve with lime wedges.

PER SERVING (3 fish cakes): 195 Cal, 5 g Fat, 1 g Sat Fat, 0 g Trans Fat, 166 mg Chol, 790 mg Sod, 11 g Carb, 1 g Fib, 26 g Prot, 57 mg Calc. **POINTS** value: **4.**

◆ Filling Extra
Mash 1 pound cooked scrubbed small red potatoes with 1/2 cup hot fat-free milk and salt and pepper to taste. The **POINTS** value for each serving will increase by **2.**

# Falafel Patties with Avocado-Lime Sauce

prep 10 min   cook 10 min   serves 4

$^1/_2$   **small Hass avocado, halved, pitted, and peeled**

2   **tablespoons fat-free sour cream**

2   **tablespoons chopped tomato**

1   **tablespoon minced red onion**

1   **teaspoon lime juice**

$^1/_4$   **teaspoon salt**

1   **(15$^1/_2$-ounce) can pinto beans, rinsed and drained**

$^1/_4$   **cup shredded fat-free Monterey Jack cheese**

$^1/_4$   **cup plain dried bread crumbs**

2   **scallions, thinly sliced**

2   **tablespoons chopped fresh cilantro**

1   **large egg white, lightly beaten**

$^1/_4$   **teaspoon ground cumin**

2   **teaspoons canola oil**

2   **(7-inch) whole-wheat pitas**

1 To make the sauce, mash the avocado in a small bowl. Add the sour cream, tomato, onion, lime juice and salt, stirring to combine well.

2 Mash the beans in a large bowl. Add the Monterey Jack, bread crumbs, scallions, cilantro, egg white, and cumin, stirring to mix well. With damp hands, form the mixture into 4 ($^1/_2$-inch-thick) oval patties.

3 Heat the oil in a large nonstick skillet over medium-high heat. Add the patties and cook until browned and crispy, about 3 minutes on each side.

4 Cut off the top third of each pita and reserve for another use. Stuff each pita with a falafel patty and top with about 2 tablespoons of the avocado sauce.

PER SERVING (1 falafel sandwich): 309 Cal, 7 g Fat, 1 g Sat Fat, 0 g Trans Fat, 2 mg Chol, 615 mg Sod, 50 g Carb, 11 g Fib, 15 g Prot, 133 mg Calc. **POINTS** value: **6.**

◆ Filling Extra

Stuff a hefty dose of your favorite micro (mini) greens or sprouts into the pitas to make this sandwich even more satisfying.

# Capellini Cake with Caramelized Onion

prep 5 min   cook 25 min   serves 8

| | |
|---|---|
| 1 | pound whole-wheat capellini |
| 2 | teaspoons vegetable oil |
| 1 | large onion, sliced |
| ¼ | cup chopped fresh parsley |
| ¼ | cup grated Parmesan cheese |
| ½ | teaspoon salt |
| ¼ | teaspoon black pepper |

1 Cook the pasta according to the package directions, omitting the salt if desired. Drain.

2 Heat 1 teaspoon of the oil in a large nonstick skillet over medium-high heat. Add the onion and cook, stirring, until softened and deep golden, about 10 minutes. Transfer the onion to a medium bowl and toss with parsley.

3 Put the pasta in a large bowl and lightly spray with nonstick spray; toss well. Add all but ⅓ cup of the onion mixture, the Parmesan, salt, and pepper: toss to combine well. Transfer the pasta mixture to the skillet and press with a spatula to form a flat cake. Reduce the heat to medium and cook until golden brown and crusty, about 15 minutes. Place a large platter or baking sheet on top of the skillet and invert the skillet. Add the remaining 1 teaspoon oil to the skillet. Slide the pasta cake back into the skillet and cook until crusty, about 5 minutes longer. Slide the pasta cake onto a platter and top with the remaining onion mixture. Cut into 8 wedges.

PER SERVING (1 wedge): 236 Cal, 3 g Fat, 1 g Sat Fat, 0 g Trans Fat, 2 mg Chol, 416 mg Sod, 46 g Carb, 5 g Fib, 10 g Prot, 74 mg Calc. **POINTS** value: **4.**

**CAPELLINI CAKE WITH CARAMELIZED ONION**

# Spice it Up

# Kick-It-Up Guacamole

prep 10 min   cook none   serves 8 as a light bite

2   Hass avocados, halved, pitted, peeled, and cut into ¹/₂-inch pieces

¹/₃   cup mild or medium chunky fat-free salsa

3   tablespoons chopped fresh cilantro

2   teaspoons lime juice

¹/₈   teaspoon ground cumin

¹/₈   teaspoon salt

Coarsely mash the avocados in a medium bowl. Add the remaining ingredients and stir until combined. If not serving right way, press a piece of plastic wrap directly onto the surface to prevent the guacamole from browning. Refrigerate up to 4 hours.

PER SERVING (¹/₄ cup): 60 Cal, 5 g Fat, 1 g Sat, 0 g Trans Fat, 0 mg Chol, 103 mg Sod, 4 g Carb, 3 g Fib, 1 g Prot, 8 mg Calc. *POINTS* value: *1.*

## So Satisfying

This temptingly chunky guacamole has just the right combination of buttery, nutty flavor (from the ripe avocados), tartness (from the lime juice) and heat (from the salsa) making it the perfect snack. Generously cut pieces of colorful bell peppers make the perfect dippers. **This recipe works with the Simply Filling technique.**

# Fennel and Orange–Marinated Olives

prep 10 min    cook none    serves 6 as a light bite

½   **pound brine-cured black and/or green olives**

2   **(2-inch) strips orange peel, removed with a vegetable peeler**

1   **garlic clove, crushed with the side of a large knife**

½   **teaspoon extra-virgin olive oil**

⅛   **teaspoon fennel seeds, crushed**

**Generous pinch red pepper flakes**

1 Stir together all the ingredients in a medium bowl. Refrigerate, covered, for at least 1 day or up to 1 week.

2 Discard the garlic; transfer the olives to a serving bowl. Serve at room temperature.

**PER SERVING** (about 4 olives): 43 Cal, 4 g Fat, 1 g Sat Fat, 0 g Trans Fat, 0 mg Chol, 387 mg Sod, 2 g Carb, 1 g Fib, 0 g Prot, 23 mg Calc. **POINTS** value: **1.**

## In the Kitchen
You can use pitted or unpitted olives with equal success here. If you do use unpitted olives, be sure to set out a small dish for the pits. This recipe works with the Simply Filling technique.

# Grilled Buffalo-Style Chicken Bites

prep 10 min   cook 5 min   serves 2 as a light bite

| | |
|---|---|
| 1 | (5-ounce) skinless boneless chicken breast |
| 2 | teaspoons Louisiana-style hot sauce |
| 1 | teaspoon canola oil |
| 1/8 | teaspoon salt |
| 2 | celery stalks |
| 1/4 | cup plain fat-free yogurt |
| 1 | tablespoon crumbled reduced-fat blue cheese |
| 1 | teaspoon chopped fresh parsley |

1 Remove the tender from the chicken breast and cut lengthwise in half. Cut the rest of the chicken breast on a long diagonal into 6 thin strips. Toss together the chicken, hot sauce, oil, and salt in a medium bowl until coated.

2 Cut the celery lengthwise in half, then crosswise into thirds to make a total of 12 celery sticks. Stir together the yogurt and blue cheese in a serving dish.

3 Thread the chicken strips on 8 (8- to 10-inch) metal skewers (if using wooden skewers, soak in water 30 minutes). Spray a nonstick ridged grill pan with nonstick spray and set over medium heat. Place the skewers on the pan and cook the chicken just until cooked through, about 2 minutes on each side.

4 Arrange the blue cheese dressing, celery sticks, and chicken skewers on a platter. Sprinkle the dressing with the parsley.

PER SERVING (4 skewers, 2 1/2 tablespoons blue cheese dressing, and 6 celery sticks): 143 Cal, 5 g Fat, 1 g Sat Fat, 0 g Trans Fat, 47 mg Chol, 292 mg Sod, 4 g Carb, 1 g Fib, 19 g Prot, 104 mg Calc. **POINTS** value: **3.**

## So Satisfying

If you thought Buffalo-style chicken was off limits because of its high fat and calorie content, think again! Satisfy your hankering for heat and cheese while keeping it lean with these winning skewers.

**GRILLED BUFFALO-STYLE CHICKEN BITES AND FENNEL AND ORANGE–MARINATED OLIVES, PAGE 93**

# Almost-Instant Jerk Shrimp

prep 5 min   cook 5 min   serves 2 as a light bite

---

| | |
|---|---|
| ½ | **pound medium shrimp (about 14), shells left on** |
| 2 | **teaspoons canola oil** |
| ¾ | **teaspoon sugar-free jerk seasoning** |
| 2 | **teaspoons chopped fresh flat-leaf parsley** |
| **Lime wedges** | |

1 Toss together the shrimp, oil, and jerk seasoning in a medium bowl until evenly coated. Let stand at room temperature, 10 minutes, stirring occasionally.

2 Meanwhile, spray a nonstick ridged grill pan with nonstick spray and set over medium-high heat. Place the shrimp on the pan and grill until just opaque throughout, about 2 minutes on each side.

3 Arrange the shrimp on a serving plate and sprinkle with the parsley. Serve with lime wedges.

PER SERVING (about 7 shrimp): 99 Cal, 5 g Fat, 1 g Sat Fat, 0 g Trans Fat, 107 mg Chol, 127 mg Sod, 1 g Carb, 1 g Fib, 12 g Prot, 32 mg Calc. **POINTS** value: **2.**

◆ Filling Extra

This shrimp dish really hits the spot when it comes to lip-tingling heat. Turn it into a meal by serving with 2 grilled bell peppers, thickly sliced, and a bowl of brown rice (½ cup cooked brown rice for each serving will increase the **POINTS** value by **2**). This recipe works with the Simply Filling technique.

# Fiery Gazpacho

prep 15 min   cook none   serves 4

1   (14$\frac{1}{2}$-ounce) can petite diced
    tomatoes
1   cup reduced-sodium vegetable
    broth
$\frac{1}{2}$   orange or yellow bell pepper,
    cut into $\frac{1}{4}$-inch dice
$\frac{1}{2}$   cup ($\frac{1}{4}$-inch) diced English
    (seedless) cucumber
$\frac{1}{2}$   small red onion, finely chopped
$\frac{1}{2}$   (4$\frac{1}{2}$-ounce) can chopped
    green chiles
1$\frac{1}{2}$   teaspoons red-wine vinegar
$\frac{1}{4}$   teaspoon salt
$\frac{1}{8}$   teaspoon cayenne

Stir together all the ingredients in a large bowl.
Refrigerate, covered, until thoroughly chilled, about
6 hours. Or place in the freezer for about 3 hours,
stirring occasionally and checking to make sure the
soup doesn't begin to freeze.

PER SERVING (1 cup): 32 Cal, 0 g Fat, 0 g Sat Fat, 0 g Trans Fat,
0 mg Chol, 470 mg Sod, 7 g Carb, 2 g Fib, 1 g Prot, 43 mg Calc.
**POINTS** value: **0.**

## In the Kitchen
Gazpacho is best enjoyed when refreshingly cold. An easy way to do this in
record time is to chill the soup bowls in the freezer while preparing the soup and
to use well-chilled cans of tomatoes and broth. This recipe works with the
Simply Filling technique.

# 15-Minute Thai Shrimp-Mushroom Soup

prep 10 min    cook 5 min    serves 4

| | |
|---|---|
| 2 | cups reduced-sodium chicken broth |
| 1 | tablespoon Thai green curry paste |
| 1 | (15-ounce) can straw mushrooms, drained |
| 1 | teaspoon Asian fish sauce |
| 1/2 | pound medium shrimp, peeled and deveined |
| 1/2 | cup frozen peas, thawed |
| 1/3 | cup lightly packed fresh cilantro leaves |

1 Whisk together the broth and curry paste in a medium saucepan; set over medium heat. Cook, whisking constantly, 1 minute.

2 Stir in the mushrooms and fish sauce; bring to a simmer over high heat. Stir in the shrimp and cook, stirring occasionally, until just opaque throughout, about 2 minutes. Stir in the peas and cook, stirring occasionally, just until heated through, about 1 minute longer. Ladle the soup evenly into 2 bowls and serve sprinkled with the cilantro.

PER SERVING (1 cup): 82 Cal, 1 g Fat, 0 g Sat Fat, 0 g Trans Fat, 53 mg Chol, 773 mg Sod, 7 g Carb, 3 g Fib, 12 g Prot, 41 mg Calc. **POINTS** value: **1.**

## In the Kitchen

Thai green curry paste is a perfect pantry item—without any extra work or trips to the supermarket, you can add the flavors of green chile, garlic, lemongrass, shallots, Kaffir lime, cumin, and coriander to the dish of your choice. The paste is available in Asian grocery markets and many supermarkets.

# Moroccan Orange–Mint Leaf Salad

prep 10 min   cook none   serves 2

2   naval oranges

1   small red onion, thinly sliced

$^1/_2$   teaspoon ground cumin

$^1/_4$   teaspoon paprika

$^1/_4$   teaspoon salt

Pinch cayenne

5   fresh mint leaves, very thinly sliced

1 With a sharp knife, remove the peel and white pith from the oranges and discard. Cut each orange crosswise into 4 slices and arrange on a platter. Scatter the onion on top.

2 Stir together the cumin, paprika, salt, and cayenne in a cup. Sprinkle over the oranges and top with the mint.

PER SERVING (4 orange slices): 76 Cal, 0 g Fat, 0 g Sat Fat, 0 g Trans Fat, 0 mg Chol, 296 mg Sod, 19 g Carb, 4 g Fib, 2 g Prot, 61 mg Calc. **POINTS** value: **1.**

◆ Filling Extra
Serve this refreshing salad on a bed of your favorite salad greens. This recipe works with the Simply Filling technique.

**LOTS OF MUSHROOMS HOT-AND-SOUR SOUP**

# Lots of Mushrooms Hot-and-Sour Soup

prep 20 min   cook 10 min   serves 8

5   cups reduced-sodium chicken broth

2   tablespoons + 1½ teaspoons cornstarch

2   (5-ounce) skinless boneless chicken breasts, cut into thin strips

1½  tablespoons reduced-sodium soy sauce

10  shiitake mushrooms, stems removed and caps thinly sliced

6   ounces firm reduced-fat tofu, drained and cut into ½-inch cubes

3   tablespoons cider vinegar

1   tablespoon + 1 teaspoon minced peeled fresh ginger

1½  teaspoons Asian (dark) sesame oil

¾   teaspoon coarsely ground black pepper

3   large egg whites, lightly beaten

1   cup lightly packed fresh cilantro leaves

1 Stir together 2 tablespoons of the broth and 1½ teaspoons of the cornstarch in a medium bowl until smooth. Add the chicken and ½ tablespoon of the soy sauce; stir until the chicken is well coated. Stir together the remaining 2 tablespoons cornstarch and 2 tablespoons chicken broth in a cup until smooth.

2 Bring the remaining 4¾ cups broth to a boil over high heat in a Dutch oven. Add the chicken mixture and the mushrooms; return to a boil. Boil 1 minute, stirring occasionally. Add the tofu and the remaining 1 tablespoon soy sauce; return to a boil, stirring occasionally. Add the remaining cornstarch mixture and cook, stirring constantly, until the soup bubbles and thickens, about 30 seconds. Stir in the vinegar, ginger, sesame oil, and pepper.

3 Remove the Dutch oven from the heat and add the egg whites in a slow, steady stream, stirring the soup once in a clockwise motion. Stir in ½ cup of the cilantro. Ladle the soup evenly into 6 soup bowls and serve sprinkled with the remaining ½ cup cilantro.

PER SERVING (1 cup): 115 Cal, 3 g Fat, 1 g Sat Fat, 0 g Trans Fat, 22 mg Chol, 490 mg Sod, 8 g Carb, 1 g Fib, 14 g Prot, 32 mg Calc. **POINTS** value: **2.**

◆ Filling Extra
Stirring 2 cups cooked brown rice into the soup along with the cilantro turns it into a satisfying lunch dish. The **POINTS** value for each serving will increase by **2.**

# Coconut Green Beans

prep 15 min  cook 10 min  serves 4

| | |
|---|---|
| 1 | pound green beans, trimmed |
| 1 | tablespoon canola oil |
| 1 | red onion, thinly sliced |
| 1 | garlic clove, minced |
| 1/4 | teaspoon salt |
| 1/8 | teaspoon cayenne |
| 1/4 | cup unsweetened shredded coconut |

1 Bring a large saucepan of water to a boil over medium-high heat. Add the green beans and cook until bright green and crisp-tender, about 5 minutes; drain.

2 Meanwhile, heat the oil in a large nonstick skillet over medium-high heat. Add the onion, garlic, salt, and cayenne; cook, stirring frequently, until the onions are softened, about 5 minutes. Add the coconut and cook, stirring constantly, until lightly browned, about 1 minute. Add the green beans and cook, stirring constantly, until heated through, about 1 minute longer.

PER SERVING (about 1 cup): 106 Cal, 7 g Fat, 3 g Sat Fat, 0 g Trans Fat, 0 mg Chol, 156 mg Sod, 11 g Carb, 5 g Fib, 3 g Prot, 46 mg Calc. **POINTS** value: **2.**

# Stir-Fried Sweet 'n' Spicy Cabbage

prep 10 min   cook 10 min   serves 4

| | |
|---|---|
| 1 | tablespoon canola oil |
| 1 | tablespoon + 1 teaspoon minced peeled fresh ginger |
| 1/8 | teaspoon cayenne |
| 6 | cups thinly sliced green cabbage |
| 4 | scallions, thinly sliced |
| 1 | tablespoon seasoned rice vinegar |
| 1/4 | teaspoon sugar |

Heat the oil in a large nonstick skillet over medium heat. Add the ginger and cook, stirring constantly, until fragrant, about 1 minute. Add the cayenne and cook, stirring constantly, about 30 seconds. Add the cabbage and cook, stirring occasionally, until softened, about 8 minutes. Remove the skillet from the heat and stir in the scallions, vinegar, and sugar. Serve hot, warm, or cold.

**PER SERVING** (3/4 cup): 68 Cal, 4 g Fat, 0 g Sat Fat, 0 g Trans Fat, 0 mg Chol, 22 mg Sod, 8 g Carb, 3 g Fib, 2 g Prot, 54 mg Calc. **POINTS** value: **1.**

◆ Filling Extra
Add 1 or 2 shredded carrots to the skillet along with the cabbage for some bright color, a bit of crunch, and good-for-you fiber and vitamins.

# Ripe Nectarine and Toasted Pepita Salad

prep 15 min   cook none   serves 4

3   small shallots, thinly sliced

1   tablespoon + 2 teaspoons cider vinegar

2   teaspoons olive oil

2   teaspoons water

³/₄  teaspoon ground coriander

¹/₂  teaspoon salt

¹/₈  teaspoon cayenne

1   large nectarine or 2 small plums, halved, pitted, and cut into thin wedges

1   head romaine lettuce, cut crosswise into 1-inch-wide strips (about 7 cups)

¹/₂  small red onion, thinly sliced

¹/₄  cup coarsely crumbled fat-free feta cheese

1¹/₂ tablespoons pepitas (pumpkin seeds) or sliced almonds, toasted

1 To make the dressing, whisk together the shallots, vinegar, oil, water, coriander, salt, and cayenne in a large bowl.

2 Add the nectarine to the dressing and gently toss to coat. Let stand 10 minutes, stirring occasionally. Add the lettuce and onion; gently toss to combine. Divide the salad evenly among 4 plates and sprinkle with the feta and pepitas.

PER SERVING (1³/₄ cups): 116 Cal, 5 g Fat, 1 g Sat Fat, 0 g Trans Fat, 1 mg Chol, 424 mg Sod, 14 g Carb, 4 g Fib, 6 g Prot, 92 mg Calc. **POINTS** value: **2.**

## So Satisfying

The combination of juicy ripe nectarine, salty feta cheese, crunchy roasted pepitas (pumpkin seeds), and lots of crisp romaine lettuce makes this salad superbly satisfying. Serve it as the first course of a grilled chicken or fajita dinner.

**RIPE NECTARINE AND TOASTED PEPITA SALAD**

# Skillet-Cooked Okra with Onion and Red Chile

prep 5 min   cook 10 min   serves 4

1   tablespoon canola oil

1   red onion, thinly sliced

1   small dried red chile or red pepper flakes to taste

1   garlic clove, minced

3/4   teaspoon ground cumin

1/2   teaspoon salt

2   (10-ounce) packages frozen cut okra, thawed

Heat the oil in a large nonstick skillet over medium-high heat. Add the onion, chile, and garlic; cook, stirring frequently, until the onion begins to soften, about 3 minutes. Add the cumin and salt; cook, stirring constantly, until fragrant, about 30 seconds. Add the okra and cook, stirring constantly, until crisp-tender, about 5 minutes longer. Discard the chile.

PER SERVING (1 cup): 81 Cal, 4 g Fat, 1 g Sat Fat, 0 g Trans Fat, 0 mg Chol, 302 mg Sod, 11 g Carb, 4 g Fib, 3 g Prot, 134 mg Calc. **POINTS** value: **1**.

## So Satisfying

Not a fan of okra? You may well be after trying this jazzed-up version. A dried red chile and a touch of fragrant cumin breathes new life into the vegetable. The trick here is to cook the okra, a mainstay of Southern cooking, only until crisp-tender. Cooking it any longer will turn it gelatinous. This recipe works with the Simply Filling technique.

# Devilish Tomatoes

prep 10 min   bake 20 min   serves 4

4   plum tomatoes (4 ounces each), halved lengthwise

¼   cup plain dried bread crumbs

2   tablespoons grated Parmesan cheese

1   tablespoon finely chopped fresh parsley

1   teaspoon dry mustard

¼   teaspoon salt

⅛   teaspoon cayenne

1 Preheat the oven to 400°F.

2 Cut a small slice off the bottom of each tomato half.

3 Stir together all the remaining ingredients in a small bowl. Mound the mixture evenly on the cut sides of the tomatoes.

4 Place the tomatoes in heavy medium ovenproof skillet or baking dish. Bake until the tomatoes are softened and the topping is browned, about 25 minutes. Serve hot.

PER SERVING (2 tomato halves): 62 Cal, 2 g Fat, 1 g Sat Fat, 0 g Trans Fat, 2 mg Chol, 254 mg Sod, 9 g Carb, 2 g Fib, 3 g Prot, 68 mg Calc. **POINTS** value: **1.**

◆ Filling Extra

Turn this tomato dish into a tempting first course by serving the tomatoes—still slightly warm—on a bed of greens, such as tender watercress sprigs, mixed baby salad greens, baby arugula, or red and green baby romaine.

# Zucchini Mexican Style

prep 10 min   cook 15 min   serves 4

- 1   tablespoon olive oil
- 1   red onion, thinly sliced
- 2   zucchini, cut on a diagonal into thick matchsticks
- 1/2   cup corn kernels (from 1 ear of corn)
- 1   (4 1/2-ounce) can chopped green chiles, drained
- 1/4   teaspoon salt
- 1/4   cup shredded reduced-fat Monterey Jack cheese

1 Heat the oil in a large nonstick skillet over medium heat. Add the onion and cook, stirring frequently, until it begins to soften, about 4 minutes. Add the zucchini. Increase the heat to medium-high and cook, stirring frequently, until it begins to soften, about 4 minutes.

2 Stir in the corn, chiles, and salt; cook, stirring occasionally, until heated through, about 3 minutes longer. Serve sprinkled with the Monterey Jack.

PER SERVING (2/3 cup zucchini mixture and 1 tablespoon cheese): 98 Cal, 5 g Fat, 2 g Sat Fat, 0 g Trans Fat, 5 mg Chol, 314 mg Sod, 11 g Carb, 2 g Fib, 4 g Prot, 80 mg Calc. **POINTS** value: **2.**

## So Satisfying

Take a quick trip across the border without leaving home with this classic side dish, which is known in Mexico as *calabacitas.* In our recipe, we use canned green chiles for a fast and easy way to get a heat fix.

# Lemon-Pepper Chickpeas

prep 20 min   cook none   serves 4

2   (15½-ounce) cans chickpeas, rinsed and drained

1   cup halved grape or cherry tomatoes

⅓   cup chopped fresh flat-leaf parsley

1   teaspoon olive oil

1   teaspoon grated lemon zest

1   tablespoon lemon juice

½   teaspoon salt

½   teaspoon cracked black pepper

4   cups lightly packed baby spinach or mixed baby salad greens

Stir together all the ingredients except the spinach in a large bowl. Divide the spinach evenly among 4 plates and top evenly with the chickpea mixture.

**PER SERVING** (generous 1 cup chickpea mixture and 1 cup spinach): 284 Cal, 6 g Fat, 0 g Trans Fat, 0 mg Chol, 535 mg Sod, 45 g Carb, 11 g Fib, 15 g Prot, 117 mg Calc. **POINTS** value: **5.**

◆ Filling Extra

Turn this tempting bean salad into a meatless main dish by serving it over warm cooked whole-wheat couscous (⅔ cup of couscous per serving will increase the **POINTS** value by **2**). This recipe works with the Simply Filling technique.

SZECHUAN PEANUT NOODLES

# Szechuan Peanut Noodles

prep 20 min   cook 15 min   serves 6

8   ounces multigrain or whole-wheat spaghetti

¹/₃   cup reduced-fat creamy peanut butter

6   tablespoons water

3   tablespoons hoisin sauce

1   tablespoon reduced-sodium soy sauce

1   tablespoon seasoned rice vinegar

¹/₂   teaspoon Asian (dark) sesame oil

Pinch cayenne

1   small yellow bell pepper, finely chopped

¹/₂   English (seedless) cucumber, halved, seeded, and finely diced

2   scallions, thinly sliced

1 Cook the pasta according to the package directions, omitting the salt if desired. Drain, then rinse under cold water. Drain again.

2 Whisk together the peanut butter, water, hoisin sauce, soy sauce, vinegar, sesame oil, and cayenne in a small saucepan until smooth; bring the mixture to a boil over medium heat.

3 Transfer the peanut sauce to a serving bowl. Add the pasta and toss to coat. Add the bell pepper and cucumber; toss well. Serve sprinkled with the scallions.

PER SERVING (about 1¹/₃ cups): 271 Cal, 7 g Fat, 1 g Sat Fat, 0 g Trans Fat, 0 mg Chol, 454 mg Sod, 46 g Carb, 4 g Fib, 13 g Prot, 32 mg Calc. *POINTS* value: **5.**

In the Kitchen

Make quick work of tossing the pasta with the sauce and the vegetables by using spring-loaded tongs.

# Mexican-Style Beans with Cilantro and Cheese

prep 10 min   cook 5 min   serves 4

1½ teaspoons canola oil

4 scallions, thinly sliced

1 garlic clove, minced

1 teaspoon ground coriander

½ teaspoon ground cumin

¼ teaspoon salt

¼ teaspoon red pepper flakes or to taste

2 (15½-ounce) cans red kidney beans, rinsed and drained

½ cup lightly packed fresh cilantro leaves

¼ cup shredded Monterey Jack cheese

Heat the oil in a large nonstick skillet over medium heat. Add the scallions and garlic; cook, stirring frequently, until the scallions are softened, about 1 minute. Stir in the coriander, cumin, salt, and red pepper flakes; cook, stirring constantly until fragrant, about 30 seconds. Stir in the beans and cook, stirring occasionally, until heated through, about 3 minutes longer. Stir in the cilantro. Served topped with the Monterey Jack.

PER SERVING (¾ cup): 247 Cal, 5 g Fat, 2 g Sat Fat, 0 g Trans Fat, 6 mg Chol, 551 mg Sod, 37 g Carb, 10 g Fib, 15 g Prot, 128 mg Calc. **POINTS** value: **5.**

## So Satisfying

This cheesy bean dish—on the table in less than 20 minutes—is sure to keep 'em coming back for more. Serve it alongside grilled chicken breasts or salmon and a plate of thickly sliced ripe tomatoes and cucumbers.

# Filet Mignon with Red Chile Onions

prep 15 min   cook 15 min   serves 4

| | |
|---|---|
| 4 | ('/4-pound) filets mignons, 3/4 inch thick, trimmed |
| 1/4 | teaspoon salt |
| 2 | teaspoons canola oil |
| 2 | red onions, thinly sliced |
| 2 | small dried red chiles |
| 2 | teaspoons minced peeled fresh ginger |
| 1 | garlic clove, minced |
| 1/4 | teaspoon fennel seeds |
| 1/2 | cup reduced-sodium vegetable broth |
| 2 | teaspoons red-wine vinegar |
| 2 | cups hot cooked brown basmati rice |

1 Sprinkle the beef with the salt. Heat the oil in a large heavy skillet over medium-high heat. Add the beef and cook until an instant-read thermometer inserted into the side of a steak registers 145°F for medium-rare, about 4 minutes on each side. Transfer to a plate.

2 Add the onions, chiles, ginger, and garlic to the skillet; cook, stirring frequently, until the onions begin to soften, about 3 minutes. Stir in the fennel seeds and cook, stirring constantly, until fragrant, about 30 seconds. Stir in the broth and vinegar; increase the heat to high and cook, stirring frequently, until most of the liquid is evaporated, about 4 minutes longer.

3 Transfer 1 filet to each of 4 plates. Stir any accumulated juices into the skillet. Discard the chiles. Top the filets evenly with the onion mixture and serve with the rice.

PER SERVING (1 filet mignon, 1/4 cup onions, and 1/2 cup rice): 329 Cal, 11 g Fat, 3 g Sat Fat, 0 g Trans Fat, 46 mg Chol, 495 mg Sod, 30 g Carb, 5 g Fib, 28 g Prot, 34 mg Calc. *POINTS* value: **7.**

## So Satisfying

Oftentimes when you're yearning for a spicy dish, it isn't just heat that you're looking for—it's the heat from a particular food, such as fresh ginger. In this recipe fennel seeds add another layer of flavor, which makes this dish even more satisfying.
This recipe works with the Simply Filling technique.

# Jerk Pork with Grilled Pineapple and Nectarines

prep 15 min   grill 5 min   serves 4

| |
|---|
| $^1/_3$   cup lightly packed fresh cilantro leaves |
| 2   scallions, sliced |
| 1   ($^1/_2$-inch) piece peeled fresh ginger |
| 1   large garlic clove, peeled |
| 2   teaspoons canola oil |
| $^1/_4$   teaspoon dried thyme |
| $^1/_4$   teaspoon salt |
| $^1/_8$   teaspoon ground allspice |
| $^1/_8$   teaspoon cayenne |
| 4   ($^1/_4$-pound) boneless center-cut pork chops, trimmed |
| 4   ($^1/_2$-inch) slices peeled fresh pineapple, cored |
| 2   firm-ripe nectarines, halved and pitted |

1 Spray the grill rack with nonstick spray. Preheat the grill to medium or prepare a medium fire.

2 Combine the cilantro, scallions, ginger, garlic, oil, thyme, salt, allspice, and cayenne in a food processor; pulse until the mixture forms a paste.

3 Place the pork, pineapple, and nectarines on the grill rack. Grill the pork, brushing both sides with the cilantro mixture, until an instant-read thermometer inserted into the side of a chop registers 160°F for medium, about 2$^1/_2$ minutes on each side. Grill the pineapple and nectarines until tender and well marked, about 2$^1/_2$ minutes on each side.

4 Divide the pork chops, pineapple, and nectarines evenly among 4 plates.

PER SERVING (1 pork chop, 1 pineapple slice, and $^1/_2$ nectarine): 268 Cal, 11 g Fat, 3 g Sat Fat, 0 g Trans Fat, 72 mg Chol, 193 mg Sod, 16 g Carb, 2 g Fib, 26 g Prot, 26 mg Calc.
***POINTS*** value: **6.**

## So Satisfying

Grilled sweet-tart nectarines and ripe pineapple are the perfect counterpoint to the temptingly spicy homemade jerk seasoning paste. Make up a big batch and use it to slather on skinless, boneless chicken breasts or trimmed pork tenderloins.
This recipe works with the Simply Filling technique.

# New Mexico–Style Green Chile Stew

prep 10 min   cook 20 min   serves 4

2    teaspoons olive oil

1    red onion, thinly sliced

1    garlic clove, crushed with the side of a large knife

4    (¼-pound) boneless center-cut pork loin chops, trimmed and cut into ¾-inch pieces

¼    teaspoon salt

⅛    teaspoon black pepper

1½   cups reduced-sodium vegetable broth

10   baby red potatoes (8 ounces), quartered

1    (4½-ounce) can chopped green chiles

¾    cup lightly packed fresh cilantro leaves

1 Heat the oil in a large heavy saucepan over medium heat. Add the onion and garlic; cook, stirring frequently, until the onion is softened, about 5 minutes. Add the pork, salt, and pepper; cook, stirring frequently, just until the pork is no longer pink, about 3 minutes. With a slotted spoon, transfer the pork to a plate.

2 Add the broth, potatoes, and chiles to the saucepan; increase the heat to medium-high and bring to a boil. Reduce the heat and simmer, covered, stirring occasionally, until the potatoes are fork-tender, about 10 minutes. Discard the garlic. Return the pork to the saucepan; cook, stirring constantly, until heated through, about 1 minute longer. Stir in ½ cup of the cilantro.

3 Ladle the stew evenly into 4 bowls. Serve sprinkled with the remaining ¼ cup cilantro.

PER SERVING (generous 1 cup): 269 Cal, 11 g Fat, 3 g Sat Fat, 0 g Trans Fat, 72 mg Chol, 391 mg Sod, 15 g Carb, 2 g Fib, 26 g Prot, 38 mg Calc. **POINTS** value: **6.**

◆ Filling Extra
Serve the stew with a bowl of steamed broccoli florets sprinkled with a pinch of red pepper flakes. This recipe works with the Simply Filling technique.

# Hoisin Beef and Shiitake Stir-Fry

prep 15 min    cook 5 min    serves 4

1    cup snow peas, trimmed

¹/₃    cup reduced-sodium beef broth

1    teaspoon cornstarch

1    tablespoon peanut or canola oil

1    large red onion, thinly sliced

2    garlic cloves, minced

Pinch red pepper flakes

4    ounces shiitake mushrooms, stems removed and caps thinly sliced

¹/₂    pound bottom round steak, trimmed and cut into long, thin strips

2    tablespoons hoisin sauce

¹/₂    teaspoon Asian (dark) sesame oil

2    cups hot cooked brown rice

1 Bring a large saucepan of water to a boil over high heat. Add the snow peas and cook until crisp-tender and bright green, about 4 minutes. Drain, then rinse under cold running water to stop the cooking. Drain on paper towels.

2 Stir together the broth and cornstarch in a small bowl until smooth.

3 Heat the peanut oil in a wok or large deep skillet over medium-high heat. When a drop of water sizzles in the pan add the onion, garlic, and red pepper flakes; stir-fry until the onion is softened, about 4 minutes. Add the mushrooms and stir-fry until they begin to soften, about 2 minutes. Add the beef and stir-fry just until no longer pink, about 2 minutes. Re-stir the cornstarch mixture and add to the wok along with the hoisin sauce and snow peas; stir-fry until the sauce bubbles and thickens, about 1 minute longer. Remove the wok from the heat and stir in the sesame oil. Serve with the rice.

PER SERVING (1 cup): 295 Cal, 8 g Fat, 2 g Sat Fat, 0 g Trans Fat, 42 mg Chol, 451 mg Sod, 34 g Carb, 5 g Fib, 22 g Prot, 36 mg Calc. **POINTS** value: **6.**

◆ Filling Extra

Consider adding another tasty vegetable to this already flavor-packed stir-fry along with the mushrooms in step 3: thinly sliced red bell pepper, small broccoli florets, watercress sprigs, or sliced celery all work equally well.

**HOISIN BEEF AND SHIITAKE STIR-FRY**

# Spiced Lamb with Cooling Yogurt Sauce

prep 15 min   grill 10 min   serves 4

| | |
|---|---|
| ½ | cup plain fat-free yogurt |
| ¼ | English (seedless) cucumber, halved, seeded, and thinly sliced (½ cup) |
| 1 | tablespoon thinly sliced fresh mint |
| ¼ | teaspoon + pinch salt |
| 1 | pound ground lean lamb |
| 2 | teaspoons minced peeled fresh ginger |
| 1 | garlic clove, crushed with a press |
| 1 | teaspoon ground cumin |
| ½ | teaspoon hot paprika, preferably smoked |
| 2 | cups very thinly sliced romaine lettuce leaves |

1 Spray the grill rack with nonstick spray. Preheat the grill to medium or prepare a medium fire.

2 Stir together the yogurt, cucumber, mint, and the pinch of salt in a serving bowl. Refrigerate, covered, until ready to use.

3 Mix together the lamb, ginger, garlic, cumin, paprika, and the remaining ¼ teaspoon salt in a medium bowl just until well blended. With damp hands, form the lamb mixture into 8 (½-inch-thick) oval patties. Thread one patty on each of 8 (6- to 8-inch) metal skewers.

4 Place the skewers on the grill rack and grill, turning, until the lamb is browned and cooked through, about 10 minutes. Remove the patties from the skewers. Spread the romaine on a small platter and place the lamb patties on top. Serve with the yogurt sauce.

PER SERVING (½ cup romaine, 2 lamb patties, and ¼ cup yogurt sauce): 169 Cal, 7 g Fat, 2 g Sat Fat, 0 g Trans Fat, 63 mg Chol, 294 mg Sod, 5 g Carb, 1 g Fib, 22 g Prot, 85 mg Calc. **POINTS** value: **4.**

◆ Filling Extra

A bowl of piping hot whole-wheat couscous sprinkled with a generous dose of thinly sliced scallions and mint is the perfect side (⅔ cup cooked whole-wheat couscous for each serving will increase the **POINTS** value by **2**). This recipe works with the Simply Filling technique.

# Cheesy Chicken Enchiladas with Green Sauce

prep 10 min   cook/microwave 20 min   serves 6

4   (½-pound) bone-in chicken breasts

1½ cups medium or hot salsa verde

12  (6-inch) corn tortillas

¾   cup part-skim ricotta cheese

¾   cup shredded reduced-fat Monterey Jack cheese or queso fresco

½   cup lightly packed coarsely chopped fresh cilantro

1 Place the chicken in a large deep skillet. Add enough water to cover and bring to a boil over medium-high heat. Reduce the heat and simmer 15 minutes. Transfer the chicken to a cutting board. When cool enough to handle, remove the skin and bones and discard; shred the chicken.

2 Spray a 9 x 13-inch baking dish with nonstick spray.

3 Put the salsa in a large shallow bowl or pie plate. Dip both sides of 1 tortilla in the salsa. Top the tortilla with about 1/4 cup of the shredded chicken, 1 tablespoon of the ricotta, and 1/2 tablespoon of the Monterey Jack. Fold two opposite sides of the tortilla over to enclose the filling. Place, seam side down, in the prepared baking dish. Repeat.

4 Pour any remaining salsa over the enchiladas and sprinkle evenly with the remaining Monterey Jack. Cover with plastic wrap and vent one corner. Microwave on High until the cheese is melted and the enchiladas are heated through, about 5 minutes. Sprinkle with the cilantro.

PER SERVING (2 enchiladas): 342 Cal, 11 g Fat, 5 g Sat Fat, 0 g Trans Fat, 85 mg Chol, 439 mg Sod, 27 g Carb, 4 g Fib, 34 g Prot, 242 mg Calc. **POINTS** value: **7.**

## In the Kitchen
If your microwave isn't large enough to hold the baking dish on its turntable, simply remove the turntable and turn the dish once during the cooking time.

**THAI CHICKEN-COCONUT CURRY**

# Thai Chicken-Coconut Curry

prep 5 min   cook 20 min   serves 4

1   cup light coconut milk

3   scallions, thinly sliced

2   tablespoons Thai green curry paste

2   cups reduced-sodium chicken broth

1   tablespoon Asian fish sauce

2   teaspoons packed light brown sugar

Pinch salt

3/4   pound chicken cutlets, cut into long, thin strips

1   cup fresh cilantro leaves

3   cups hot cooked jasmine rice

1 Heat the coconut milk in a large heavy saucepan over medium heat. Stir in the scallions and curry paste; cook, stirring frequently, until heated through and smooth, about 3 minutes. Stir in the broth and bring to a boil over medium-high heat, stirring constantly. Reduce the heat to a simmer. Add the fish sauce, brown sugar, and salt; cook stirring occasionally, 2 minutes.

2 Add the chicken to the curry sauce and cook, stirring occasionally, until just cooked through, about 2 minutes. Stir in the cilantro. Ladle the curry evenly into deep bowls and serve with the rice.

PER SERVING (1 1/4 cups curry and 3/4 cup rice): 312 Cal, 7 g Fat, 3 g Sat Fat, 0 g Trans Fat, 51 mg Chol, 984 mg Sod, 39 g Carb, 2 g Fib, 24 g Prot, 54 mg Calc **POINTS** value: **6.**

◆ Filling Extra

Add some vegetable goodness to the curry by stirring in 1 each of a red and yellow bell pepper, thinly sliced, along with the broth in step 1.

# California Fish Tacos

prep 15 min   microwave 5 min   serves 4

| | |
|---|---|
| 1 | **tablespoon lime juice** |
| 2 | **teaspoons olive oil** |
| ³/₄ | **teaspoon chili powder** |
| ³/₄ | **teaspoon ground coriander** |
| ¹/₄ | **teaspoon salt** |
| 3 | **(¹/₄-pound) red snapper fillets** |
| 2 | **cups thinly sliced green cabbage** |
| 2 | **scallions, thinly sliced** |
| ¹/₂ | **cup finely chopped red onion** |
| ¹/₃ | **cup coarsely chopped fresh cilantro** |
| 8 | **(6-inch) corn tortillas, warmed** |

1 Spray a 7 x 11-inch baking dish with nonstick spray.

2 Stir together the lime juice, oil, chili powder, coriander, and salt in a cup. Place the fish in the prepared baking dish in one layer and brush with the lime juice mixture. Cover with plastic wrap and vent one corner. Microwave on High until the fish is just opaque in the center, about 3 minutes. Break the fish into flakes.

3 Stir together all the remaining ingredients except the tortillas in a medium bowl.

4 Top each tortilla with about 2 tablespoons of the cabbage mixture, 2 tablespoons of the fish, and another 1 tablespoon of the cabbage mixture. Fold the tortillas in half.

PER SERVING (2 tacos): 212 Cal, 5 g Fat, 1 g Sat Fat, 0 g Trans Fat, 38 mg Chol, 242 mg Sod, 27 g Carb, 4 g Fib, 17 g Prot, 79 mg Calc. **POINTS** value: **4.**

◆ Filling Extra
Serve a plate of dressed avocado wedges alongside. Halve, pit, and peel an avocado. Cut into wedges and arrange on a plate. Squeeze the juice of ¹/₂ lime over the avocado and sprinkle with salt and pepper (¹/₄ avocado for each serving will increase the **POINTS** value by **2**).

# Mussels in Spicy Tomato Sauce

prep 15 min   cook 15 min   serves 4

| | |
|---|---|
| 1 | tablespoon olive oil |
| 1 | large garlic clove, halved |
| 1 | small bay leaf |
| 1/4 | teaspoon red pepper flakes |
| 1 | (14$\frac{1}{2}$-ounce) can petite diced tomatoes |
| 1$\frac{1}{4}$ | cups tomato juice |
| 1/2 | teaspoon dried basil |
| 5 | dozen mussels, scrubbed and debearded |
| 3 | tablespoons chopped fresh parsley |

1 Heat the oil in a Dutch oven over medium heat. Add the garlic and cook, stirring frequently, until golden, about 4 minutes. Add the bay leaf and red pepper flakes; cook, stirring constantly, until fragrant, about 30 seconds.

2 Add the tomatoes, tomato juice, and basil to the Dutch oven; bring to a boil over high heat. Reduce the heat and simmer, stirring occasionally, until slightly thickened, about 5 minutes.

3 Stir in the mussels and bring to a boil over high heat. Reduce the heat and simmer, covered, until the mussels open, about 3 minutes. Discard any mussels that do not open. Discard the bay leaf and garlic. Divide the mussels and liquid evenly among 4 bowl. Serve sprinkled with the parsley

PER SERVING (15 mussels): 241 Cal, 6 g Fat, 1 g Sat Fat, 0 g Trans Fat, 82 mg Chol, 1037 mg Sod, 14 g Carb, 1 g Fib, 32 g Prot, 157 mg Calc. **POINTS** value: **5.**

◆ Filling Extra
Turn this super-tasty dish into a hearty meal by serving the mussels and sauce over whole-wheat spaghetti (1 cup cooked whole-wheat spaghetti for each serving will increase thc **POINTS** value by **3**).

# Ginger-Broiled Salmon with Cucumber-Mint Relish

prep 15 min   broil 10 min   serves 4

| | |
|---|---|
| 1 | English (seedless) cucumber, halved, seeded, and thinly sliced |
| 1/4 | cup thinly sliced fresh mint |
| 1/4 | cup seasoned rice vinegar |
| 2 1/2 | teaspoons minced peeled fresh ginger |
| 2 | teaspoons canola oil |
| 1/4 | teaspoon sugar |
| Pinch salt | |
| Pinch black pepper | |
| 4 | (6-ounce) salmon steaks, about 1 inch thick |

1 To make the relish, stir together the cucumber, mint, vinegar, and 1/2 teaspoon of the ginger in a medium bowl.

2 Preheat the broiler. Spray the broiler rack with nonstick spray.

3 Stir together the remaining 2 teaspoons ginger, the oil, sugar, salt, and pepper in a cup. Rub the ginger mixture on both sides of the salmon steaks. Place the salmon on the broiler rack and broil 4 inches from the heat until the fish is just opaque throughout, about 5 minutes on each side. Serve with the cucumber relish.

PER SERVING (1 salmon steak and 1/2 cup relish): 258 Cal, 11 g Fat, 3 g Sat Fat, 0 g Trans Fat, 95 mg Chol, 399 mg Sod, 8 g Carb, 1 g Fib, 31 g Prot, 30 mg Calc. **POINTS** value: **6.**

◆ Filling Extra
This elegant yet easy salmon dish—perfect for family or friends—tastes great with a bowl of steamed scrubbed red baby potatoes (1/4 pound cooked baby potatoes for each serving will increase the **POINTS** value by **1**).

**GINGER-BROILED SALMON WITH CUCUMBER-MINT RELISH**

# Penne Arrabbiata

prep 10 min   cook 20 min   serves 6

1   pound whole-wheat penne

1   (28-ounce) can peeled plum tomatoes

1   tablespoon extra-virgin olive oil

3   garlic cloves, minced

1/2   teaspoon red pepper flakes

1/2   cup chopped fresh flat-leaf parsley

1/2   teaspoon salt

1/3   cup grated Parmesan cheese

1 Cook the pasta according to the package directions, omitting the salt if desired. Drain and keep warm.

2 Puree the tomatoes with their juice in a blender or food processor.

3 Heat the oil in a large heavy saucepan over medium heat. Stir in the garlic and red pepper flakes; cook, stirring constantly, until fragrant, about 30 seconds. Add the pureed tomatoes, 1/4 cup of the parsley, and the salt; simmer, stirring occasionally, until thickened, about 20 minutes.

4 Transfer the pasta to a serving bowl. Add the sauce and toss to coat. Sprinkle with the remaining 1/4 cup parsley and the Parmesan.

PER SERVING (1 1/2 cups): 329 Cal, 5 g Fat, 2 g Sat Fat, 0 g Trans Fat, 4 mg Chol, 755 mg Sod, 62 g Carb, 7 g Fib, 15 g Prot, 156 mg Calc. **POINTS** value: **6.**

◆ Filling Extra
Stir 2 cups bite-size pieces of broccoli rabe or broccoli into the sauce during the last 3 minutes of cooking time in step 3.

# Cumin and Cayenne–Spiked Scrambled Eggs

prep 15 min   cook 10 min   serves 4

2    teaspoons canola oil

4    scallions, thinly sliced

2    teaspoons minced peeled
     fresh ginger

$^{1}/_{2}$   teaspoon cumin seeds

$^{1}/_{4}$   teaspoon salt

$^{1}/_{8}$   teaspoon cayenne

1    (16-ounce) container fat-free
     egg substitute

2    plum tomatoes, seeded and
     coarsely chopped

$^{1}/_{3}$   cup coarsely chopped fresh
     cilantro

1 Heat the oil in a large nonstick skillet over medium heat. Add the scallions and ginger; cook, stirring occasionally, until the scallions are softened, about 2 minutes. Add the cumin, salt, and cayenne; cook, stirring constantly, until fragrant, about 30 seconds.

2 Add the egg substitute and cook, without stirring, 2 minutes. Stir in the tomatoes and cilantro; cook, stirring occasionally, until the eggs form large, soft curds, about 2 minutes longer.

PER SERVING (1 cup): 92 Cal, 3 g Fat, 0 g Sat Fat, 0 g Trans Fat, 0 mg Chol, 386 mg Sod, 5 g Carb, 2 g Fib, 13 g Prot, 220 mg Calc. *POINTS* value: *2.*

Tip
This recipe works with the Simply Filling technique.

**GREEN CHILE AND CHEESE CORNBREAD**

# Green Chile and Cheese Cornbread

prep 15 min   bake 45 min   serves 8

1    cup yellow cornmeal, preferably
     stone ground
1    teaspoon baking powder
1/2  teaspoon baking soda
1    cup low-fat buttermilk
1/2  cup fat-free egg substitute
2    tablespoons olive oil
1    (14³/₄-ounce) can cream-style
     corn
2    (4¹/₂-ounce) cans chopped green
     chiles, drained
1/2  cup shredded reduced-fat
     Monterey Jack cheese

1 Place an oven rack in the lower third of the oven and preheat the oven to 350°F. Spray a 10-inch cast-iron or other heavy ovenproof skillet with nonstick spray.

2 Whisk together the cornmeal, baking powder, and baking soda in a large bowl. Whisk together the buttermilk, egg substitute, and oil in a medium bowl until thoroughly combined. Stir in the corn, chiles, and Monterey Jack. Add the buttermilk mixture to the cornmeal mixture and stir to combine well. Pour the batter into the skillet.

3 Bake until the cornbread is golden brown and a toothpick inserted into the center comes out clean, about 45 minutes. Let cool slightly in the pan on a wire rack. Cut into 8 wedges and serve warm.

PER SERVING (1 wedge): 191 Cal, 6 g Fat, 2 g Sat Fat, 0 g Trans Fat, 6 mg Chol, 513 mg Sod, 29 g Carb, 2 g Fib, 7 g Prot, 156 mg Calc. **POINTS** value: **4.**

## In the Kitchen
If you like your cornbread with an extra-crispy crust, preheat the skillet in the oven while preparing the batter. Be sure to check for doneness early, as the baking time may be shorter by 5 minutes or so.

# Delicious Desserts

chapter 4

# Fresh Mango with Lime Cream

prep 15 min   cook none   serves 4

½   cup fat-free Greek yogurt

3   tablespoons light sour cream

2   tablespoons sugar

½   teaspoon grated lime zest

1   tablespoon lime juice

2   mangoes, peeled, pitted, and sliced

¼   cup blueberries or raspberries

Stir together the yogurt, sour cream, sugar, and lime zest and juice in a small bowl. Arrange the mango slices on 4 dessert plates; spoon the lime cream evenly on top. Sprinkle with the blueberries.

PER SERVING (½ mango, 1 tablespoon blueberries, and about 3 tablespoons cream): 130 Cal, 2 g Fat, 1 g Sat Fat, 0 g Trans Fat, 5 mg Chol, 31 mg Sod, 28 g Carb, 2 g Fib, 3 g Prot, 87 mg Calc. **POINTS** value: **2.**

## So Satisfying

Thick and creamy smooth Greek yogurt is the perfect counterpoint to the refreshing citrus-infused cream topping. Dress this dessert up for company—without extra work—by layering the ingredients in wine goblets and garnishing each serving with a fragrant mint sprig.

# Ambrosia Cups

prep 10 min   cook none   serves 4

1   (6-ounce) container apricot-
    mango fat-free yogurt

1   (11-ounce) can mandarin
    oranges in light syrup, drained

1   (8-ounce) can pineapple chunks
    in juice, drained

1   large banana, sliced

1/3  cup miniature marshmallows

2   tablespoons sweetened flaked
    coconut, toasted

Divide the yogurt evenly among 4 dessert dishes. Gently mix together the oranges, pineapple, and banana in a medium bowl. Top the yogurt evenly with the fruit; sprinkle with the marshmallows and coconut.

**PER SERVING** (1 dessert): 158 Cal, 1 g Fat, 1 g Sat Fat, 0 g Trans Fat, 1 mg Chol, 39 mg Sod, 36 g Carb, 2 g Fib, 3 g Prot, 81 mg Calc. **POINTS** value: **3.**

◆ Filling Extra
Add some bright color to the ambrosia by mixing a 6-ounce container of raspberries into the fruit mixture in step 2.

# Sweet Cherry Bruschetta

prep 15 min   cook none   serves 4

1½ cups sweet cherries, pitted
   and halved

2   teaspoons sugar

³/₄  cup fat-free ricotta cheese

4   (½-inch) slices whole-wheat
   Italian bread, toasted

1   tablespoon honey

Stir together the cherries and sugar in a small bowl. Let stand until the sugar is dissolved, about 10 minutes. Spread the ricotta evenly over the slices of bread. Top evenly with the cherries and drizzle with the honey.

PER SERVING (1 slice bruschetta): 187 Cal, 1 g Fat, 0 g Sat Fat, 0 g Trans Fat, 3 mg Chol, 169 mg Sod, 29 g Carb, 3 g Fib, 8 g Prot, 88 mg Calc. **POINTS** value: **3.**

◆ Filling Extra

Add ½ cup sliced strawberries to the cherry mixture.

**SWEET CHERRY BRUSCHETTA**

# Ginger-Lemon Sorbet Sandwiches

prep 10 min   cook none   serves 4

1   **cup lemon sorbet, slightly
    softened**

16  **(2-inch) gingersnap cookies**

With a small ice-cream scoop or spoon, place
2 tablespoons of the sorbet on the bottom of each of
8 of the cookies. Top with the remaining cookies,
bottom side down, pressing down lightly to spread the
sorbet. Place the sandwiches on a plate in one layer.
Cover tightly with plastic wrap and freeze until the sorbet
is hard, at least 2 hours or up to 1 day.

**PER SERVING** (2 sandwiches): 183 Cal, 3 g Fat, 0 g Sat Fat,
0 g Trans Fat, 0 mg Chol, 176 mg Sod, 39 g Carb, 1 g Fib,
2 g Prot, 27 mg Calc. **POINTS** value: **4.**

## In the Kitchen

In Italy, a most-beloved treat is a brioche roll split and filled with lemon sorbet. Our
equally delicious—but much lower in calories version—is just as fabulous.

# Turkish-Style Glazed Apricots and Cherries

prep 15 min   cook 20 min   serves 4

1   cup dried California apricots
¼   cup dried tart cherries
⅔   cup orange juice
½   cup water
4   tablespoons sugar
½   cup fat-free Greek yogurt
⅛   teaspoon cinnamon
2   tablespoons unsalted
    pistachios, chopped

1 Combine the apricots, cherries, orange juice, water, and 3 tablespoons of the sugar in a medium saucepan; bring to a boil over medium-high heat. Reduce the heat and simmer, covered, until the fruit is softened, about 20 minutes. Transfer the fruit mixture to a large bowl and let stand until cool.

2 Mix together the yogurt, cinnamon, and the remaining 1 tablespoon sugar in a small bowl.

3 Place a generous ⅓ cup of the fruit mixture in each of 4 dessert dishes. Top each with 2 tablespoons yogurt mixture and 1½ teaspoons pistachios.

PER SERVING (1 dessert): 220 Cal, 2 g Fat, 0 g Sat Fat, 0 g Trans Fat, 1 mg Chol, 32 mg Sod, 49 g Carb, 4 g Fib, 4 g Prot, 97 mg Calc. **POINTS** value: **4.**

## So Satisfying

We love the color pop of the deep orange apricots, crimson cherries, and bright green pistachios, but you can also use almonds or hazelnuts if you like.

**ALMOST-INSTANT APPLE CRUMBLE À LA MODE**

# Almost-Instant Apple Crumble à la Mode

prep 20 min   microwave 5 min   serves 2

2    Granny Smith apples, peeled, halved, cored, and sliced

3    tablespoons packed brown sugar

¼    teaspoon apple pie spice

1    fat-free oatmeal-raisin cookie, crumbled

½    cup vanilla fat-free ice cream or frozen yogurt

2    (3-inch) cinnamon sticks (optional)

1 Toss together the apples, brown sugar, and apple pie spice in a medium microwavable bowl. Cover with a piece of plastic wrap and vent one corner. Microwave on High, stirring once, until the apples are softened, about 3 minutes. Uncover and microwave 1 minute longer. Let stand until warm.

2 Spoon the apple mixture evenly into 2 dessert dishes; top evenly with the cookie crumbs. Top each crumble with a 1/4-cup scoop ice cream and garnish each with a cinnamon stick if using.

**PER SERVING** (1 dessert): 218 Cal, 0 g Fat, 0 g Sat Fat, 0 g Trans Fat, 0 mg Chol, 61 mg Sod, 55 g Carb, 3 g Fib, 2 g Prot, 78 mg Calc. **POINTS** value: **4.**

## So Satisfying

When the urge for a homemade apple dessert hits, this is the recipe to turn to. The apples are warmly scented with apple pie spice, sweetened with brown sugar, and microwaved until invitingly tender. Topped with crunchy cookie crumbs and served à la mode, it's sure to hit the spot.

# Cherry-Vanilla Clafouti

prep 20 min   microwave/bake 40 min   serves 8

1   **cup low-fat (1%) milk**

1   **cup fat-free egg substitute**

²/₃   **cup all-purpose flour**

¹/₃   **cup sugar**

1   **teaspoon vanilla extract**

**Pinch salt**

1   **cup fat-free half-and-half**

1   **pound sweet cherries, pitted**

1   **tablespoon confectioners' sugar**

1 Preheat the oven to 375°F. Spray a 10-inch pie plate or 2-quart shallow baking dish with nonstick spray.

2 Pour the milk into a medium microwavable bowl. Microwave on High until hot, about 90 seconds.

3 Pour the egg substitute into a medium bowl. Gradually whisk in the flour until smooth. Whisk in the sugar, vanilla, and salt, then whisk in the half-and-half and hot milk. Spread the cherries evenly in the prepared dish; pour the batter over. Bake until a knife inserted into the center comes out clean, about 35 minutes. Dust the clafouti with the confectioners' sugar. Cut into 8 wedges and serve warm.

PER SERVING (1 wedge): 139 Cal, 1 g Fat, 0 g Sat Fat, 0 g Trans Fat, 3 mg Chol, 100 mg Sod, 30 g Carb, 1 g Fib, 4 g Prot, 80 mg Calc. **POINTS** value: **3.**

## In the Kitchen

This casual fruit-and-custard dessert from the Limousin region of France is the perfect showcase for ripe, sweet cherries, the fruit traditionally used in clafoutis. If you prefer, however, substitute sliced apricots, plums, peaches, or apples.

# Streusel-Topped Oven-Roasted Peaches

prep 10 min   bake 15 min   serves 4

4   peaches, halved and pitted

¼   cup packed brown sugar

3   tablespoons all-purpose flour

2   tablespoons slivered or whole blanched almonds, chopped

1   tablespoon unsalted butter, cut into pieces

1   cup vanilla fat-free frozen yogurt

1 Preheat the oven to 425°F.

2 Arrange the peach halves, cut side up, in a 2-quart shallow baking dish.

3 With your fingers, rub together the brown sugar, flour, almonds, and butter until a crumbly mixture forms. Top the peach halves evenly with the streusel mixture, pressing lightly so it adheres. Bake until the peaches are tender and the topping is browned, about 15 minutes. Serve warm with the frozen yogurt.

PER SERVING (2 peach halves and ¼ cup frozen yogurt): 234 Cal, 5 g Fat, 2 g Sat Fat, 0 g Trans Fat, 9 mg Chol, 39 mg Sod, 45 g Carb, 3 g Fib, 5 g Prot, 111 mg Calc. *POINTS* value: *4.*

◆ Filling Extra
Sprinkle ½ cup raspberries or sliced strawberries around each dessert.

# Melon with Lemon Syrup and Candied Ginger

prep 15 min   cook none   serves 4

2     tablespoons sugar

½     teaspoon grated lemon zest

1     tablespoon lemon juice

1     tablespoon cold water

**Small pinch cayenne**

½     large cantaloupe, seeded,
       peeled, and cut into 4 wedges

1     cup cubed seedless watermelon

1     cup cubed seeded honeydew

1     tablespoon finely chopped
       crystallized ginger

1 Stir together the sugar, lemon zest and juice, water, and cayenne in a cup. Let stand 5 minutes; stir until the sugar is dissolved.

2 Place a wedge of cantaloupe on each of 4 plates. Spoon the watermelon and honeydew cubes over and around the cantaloupe. Drizzle lemon syrup evenly over each serving and sprinkle evenly with the ginger.

PER SERVING (1 dessert): 99 Cal, 0 g Fat, 0 g Sat Fat, 0 g Trans Fat, 0 mg Chol, 29 mg Sod, 25 g Carb, 2 g Fib, 1 g Prot, 20 mg Calc. **POINTS** value: **2.**

## In the Kitchen

To shave 5 minutes off your prep time, substitute an equal amount of superfine sugar for the regular granulated sugar—it will dissolve instantly!

**MELON WITH LEMON SYRUP AND CANDIED GINGER**

# Strawberry–Angel Food Cake Trifle

prep 30 min   cook none   serves 8

1   **cup frozen tropical fruit blend, thawed**

2   **tablespoons seedless raspberry jam**

1   **cup refrigerated tapioca or rice pudding**

½   **cup French vanilla fat-free yogurt**

¾   **cup thawed frozen fat-free whipped topping**

1   **(1-pound) container strawberries**

½   **(9-ounce) angel food cake, cut into 1-inch cubes**

1 Put the fruit blend in a food processor and process until smooth. Add the raspberry jam and process until well combined.

2 Stir together the pudding and yogurt in a large bowl. Fold in 1/2 cup of the whipped topping. Reserve 4 small strawberries for garnish. Hull and slice the remaining strawberries.

3 Layer half of the cake cubes, half of the sliced strawberries, half of the fruit sauce, and half of the pudding mixture in a 2-quart footed trifle bowl or straight-sided glass bowl. Repeat the layering once. Cover the bowl tightly with plastic wrap and refrigerate until the trifle is set, at least 4 hours or up to overnight.

4 To serve, garnish the trifle with the remaining 1/4 cup whipped topping and the 4 reserved strawberries, halved.

PER SERVING (about 3/4 cup): 169 Cal, 1 g Fat, 0 g Sat Fat, 0 g Trans Fat, 2 mg Chol, 256 mg Sod, 38 g Carb, 2 g Fib, 4 g Prot, 61 mg Calc. **POINTS** value: **3.**

# Banana Split Ice-Cream Sandwiches

prep 15 min   cook 5 min   serves 4

8   (¼-inch) slices fat-free pound cake

¼   cup strawberry jam

1   cup vanilla fat-free ice cream

1   large banana, sliced

2   tablespoons fat-free chocolate sauce

1 Spray a nonstick ridged grill pan with nonstick spray and set over medium heat. Place the slices of pound cake on the pan and cook until browned, about 1½ minutes on each side.

2 Spread 1 tablespoon jam on one side of 4 slices of cake. Spread ¼ cup ice cream over each of the remaining 4 slices of cake. Place, ice cream side down, on top of the jam covered slices to make 4 sandwiches in all.

3 Place each sandwich on a dessert plate and top evenly with the banana. Drizzle evenly with the chocolate sauce and serve at once.

**PER SERVING** (1 garnished sandwich): 263 Cal, 0 g Fat, 0 g Sat Fat, 0 g Trans Fat, 0 mg Chol, 174 mg Sod, 89 g Carb, 2 g Fib, 6 g Prot, 204 mg Calc. **POINTS** value: **5.**

## So Satisfying

What can be more cooling on a hot summer's day than an icy cold ice-cream sandwich? With all the flavors of a classic soda fountain banana split, you are sure to turn to this recipe again and again. You can make the sandwiches ahead—minus the bananas and chocolate sauce—and freeze them individually wrapped.

SWEET BERRY FOCACCIA

# Sweet Berry Focaccia

prep 15 min   bake 25 min   serves 8

1   (1-pound) pizza dough, preferably whole wheat, at room temperature
1   tablespoon unsalted butter, melted
2   teaspoons olive oil
2   tablespoons granulated sugar
1   cup blueberries
1   (6-ounce) container raspberries
3   tablespoons turbinado sugar

1 Line a jelly-roll pan with parchment paper and spray with nonstick spray.

2 On a lightly floured surface, roll the dough into a 9 x 13-inch rectangle. Transfer to the prepared pan. Cover with a clean kitchen towel and let rest about 15 minutes.

3 Meanwhile, preheat the oven to 400°F.

4 Mix together the butter and oil in a cup; brush over the dough and sprinkle evenly with the granulated sugar. Sprinkle the blueberries over the dough, lightly pressing them into the dough. Sprinkle evenly with the raspberries and 2 tablespoons of the turbinado sugar.

5 Bake the focaccia until the dough is golden brown along the edges and the fruit is juicy, about 25 minutes. Slide the focaccia with the parchment onto a large wire rack (or 2 small racks placed side by side). With a spatula, separate the focaccia from the parchment; slip out the parchment and discard. Transfer the focaccia to a cutting board and sprinkle with the remaining 1 tablespoon turbinado. Cut lengthwise in half, then crosswise into 4 pieces. Serve at once.

**PER SERVING** (1 piece): 224 Cal, 6 g Fat, 3 g Sat Fat, 0 g Trans Fat, 4 mg Chol, 302 mg Sod, 40 g Carb, 6 g Fib, 7 g Prot, 91 mg Calc. **POINTS** value: **4.**

# Frozen Key Lime Pie

prep 10 min   cook none   serves 10

---

1   **(14-ounce) can fat-free sweetened condensed milk**

1   **tablespoon grated lime zest**

½   **cup lime juice**

2   **cups thawed frozen fat-free whipped topping**

1   **(6-ounce) prepared reduced-fat graham cracker crust**

1   **small lime, thinly sliced**

1 Whisk together the condensed milk and lime zest and juice in a large bowl. Fold in the whipped topping, one-third at a time, just until blended. Spoon the filling into the graham cracker crust, smoothing the top with a rubber spatula. Freeze until firm, at least 4 hours or up to 1 day.

2 To serve, let the pie stand at room temperature 10 minutes for easier slicing. Garnish each serving with a slice of lime and serve at once.

**PER SERVING** (¹/₁₀ of pie): 210 Cal, 3 g Fat, 1 g Sat Fat, 0 g Trans Fat, 2 mg Chol, 120 mg Sod, 44 g Carb, 1 g Fib, 4 g Prot, 119 mg Calc. **POINTS** value: **4.**

**FROZEN KEY LIME PIE**

# Strawberry-Mint Freeze

prep 10 min   cook none   serves 2

2   **cups strawberries, hulled**

1   **cup strawberry sorbet, slightly softened**

2   **tablespoons lightly packed fresh mint leaves**

1   **teaspoon grated lemon zest**

2   **tablespoons lemon juice**

½   **cup vanilla low-fat frozen yogurt, slightly softened**

2   **lemon slices**

2   **mint sprigs**

Put the strawberries in a blender and blend until a chunky puree forms. Add the sorbet, mint, and lemon zest and juice; blend until combined but still frozen. Add the frozen yogurt, stirring until some streaks of white remain. Pour evenly into 2 glasses and garnish each with a lemon slice and a mint sprig. Serve at once.

PER SERVING (about 1 cup): 247 Cal, 2 g Fat, 1 g Sat Fat, 0 g Trans Fat, 4 mg Chol, 52 mg Sod, 59 g Carb, 4 g Fib, 4 g Prot, 131 mg Calc. **POINTS** value: **4.**

# Peach-Raspberry Galette

prep 20 min   bake 35 min   serves 10

1   refrigerated piecrust (from a 15-ounce box), at room temperature

$1/3$   cup + 2 tablespoons sugar

1   tablespoon cornstarch

$1/2$   teaspoon grated lemon zest

$1^1/2$   pounds peaches (about 5), halved, pitted, and cut into 1-inch wedges

1   (6-ounce) container raspberries

1 Preheat the oven to 400°F. Line a large baking sheet with parchment paper.

2 On a lightly floured surface, roll the crust into a 13-inch round. Transfer to the prepared baking sheet.

3 Whisk together $1/3$ cup of the sugar, the cornstarch, and lemon zest in a large bowl. Add the peaches and toss to mix well. Gently stir in the raspberries. Spoon the filling over the crust, leaving a 2-inch border. Fold the edge of the dough over the filling, pleating it as you go around. Lightly brush the edge of the dough with water; sprinkle the edge and fruit with the remaining 2 tablespoons sugar.

4 Bake until the filling is bubbling in the center and the crust is browned, about 35 minutes. Let cool 10 minutes. Slide the galette with the parchment onto a wire rack. With a spatula, separate the galette from the parchment; slip out the parchment and discard. Let the galette cool completely. Cut into wedges.

**PER SERVING** ($1/10$ of galette): 155 Cal, 6 g Fat, 2 g Sat Fat, 0 g Trans Fat, 2 mg Chol, 112 mg Sod, 26 g Carb, 2 g Fib, 1 g Prot, 8 mg Calc. **POINTS** value: **3.**

SANGRIA SORBET AND HONEY AND CORNMEAL BUTTER COOKIES, PAGE 155

# Sangria Sorbet

prep 20 min   cook 5 min   serves 8

1   **(750-ml) bottle white zinfandel or white merlot wine**

1¼ **cups sugar**

1   **(12-ounce) bag frozen mixed berries**

1   **cup orange juice**

3   **tablespoons lime juice**

2   **tablespoons lemon juice**

1   **cup seedless grapes, halved if large**

1 Combine the wine and sugar in a large saucepan and bring to a boil over high heat; boil 1 minute. Stir in the frozen berries. Remove the saucepan from the heat; let stand 30 minutes.

2 With a slotted spoon, transfer the berries to a blender and puree. Set a sieve over the saucepan. Pour the puree through the sieve; discard the seeds. Stir in the orange juice, lime juice, and lemon juice. Pour the mixture into a shallow 2-quart baking dish. Tightly cover the dish with foil and freeze overnight. Place the grapes on a plate. Tightly wrap in foil and freeze overnight.

3 Cut the sorbet into 1-inch chunks. Put half the chunks in a food processor and process until creamy but still frozen. Spoon into a freezer container; repeat with the remaining sorbet. Freeze, covered, until hard, at least 2 hours or up to 1 day.

4 Let the sorbet soften slightly, then scoop evenly into dessert dishes and garnish with the frozen grapes. Serve at once.

**PER SERVING** (¾ cup): 190 Cal, 0 g Fat, 0 g Sat Fat, 0 g Trans Fat, 0 mg Chol, 8 mg Sod, 45 g Carb, 1 g Fib, 1 g Prot, 18 mg Calc. ***POINTS*** value: **4.**

## In the Kitchen
A light and fruity red wine, such as a beaujolais, is also a good choice here.

# Chock-Full-of-Goodness Bar Cookies

prep 15 min  bake 20 min  makes 2 dozen

1   cup quick-cooking oats
¹/₂  cup toasted wheat germ
¹/₄  cup white whole-wheat flour
¹/₂  cup dried apricots
¹/₂  cup dried figs, stems removed
¹/₂  cup raisins
¹/₂  cup whole unblanched almonds
¹/₄  cup dry-roasted sunflower seeds
¹/₄  cup dried cranberries
³/₄  teaspoon cinnamon
Pinch salt
¹/₂  cup fat-free egg substitute
¹/₃  cup pure maple syrup

1 Preheat the oven to 350°F. Line a 9 x 13-inch baking pan with foil, allowing the excess foil to extend over the rim of the pan by 2 inches. Lightly spray the foil with nonstick spray.

2 Combine the oats, wheat germ, flour, apricots, figs, raisins, almonds, sunflower seeds, dried cranberries, cinnamon, and salt in a food processor, in batches if necessary, and process until finely chopped. Add the egg substitute and maple syrup; pulse until the mixture is well blended.

3 Spoon the fruit mixture into the prepared pan and press to form an even layer. Bake until firm and browned along the edges, about 20 minutes. Let cool completely in the pan on a wire rack. Lift the bars from the pan using the foil as handles. Cut into 24 bars.

PER SERVING (1 bar): 92 Cal, 3 g Fat, 0 g Sat Fat, 0 g Trans Fat, 0 mg Chol, 29 mg Sod, 16 g Carb, 2 g Fib, 3 g Prot, 32 mg Calc. **POINTS** value: **2.**

## In the Kitchen

White whole-wheat flour can be found in large supermarkets and in specialty-foods stores. It is finely milled from a special strain of wheat known as hard white spring wheat. The resulting flour has a soft texture much like that of white flour, however, it retains all of the germ and bran, making it as nutritious as regular whole-wheat flour.

# Honey and Cornmeal Butter Cookies

prep 25 min  bake 10 min  makes 3 dozen

1    cup white whole-wheat flour*
½    cup cornmeal
½    teaspoon baking soda
¼    teaspoon salt
½    cup + 1 tablespoon sugar
2    tablespoons unsalted butter,
     softened
1    large egg
2    tablespoons olive oil
1    tablespoon honey
1    tablespoon grated lemon zest

1 Preheat the oven to 350°F. Spray 2 large baking sheets with nonstick spray.

2 Whisk together the flour, cornmeal, baking soda, and salt in a small bowl.

3 With an electric mixer on low speed, beat ½ cup of the sugar and the butter until well blended, about 2 minutes. Beat in the egg, oil, honey, and lemon zest. Add the flour mixture, about ½ cup at a time, beating just until blended.

4 Roll rounded teaspoonfuls of the dough into 1-inch balls. Place 2½ inches apart on the prepared baking sheets. Dip a fork in the remaining 1 tablespoon sugar and press a crosshatch in a cookie; repeat with the remaining cookies. Bake until golden brown along the edges, about 10 minutes. Transfer the cookies to wire racks to cool completely.

PER SERVING (1 cookie): 48 Cal, 2 g Fat, 1 g Sat Fat, 0 g Trans Fat, 8 mg Chol, 36 mg Sod, 8 g Carb, 1 g Fib, 1 g Prot, 2 mg Calc. **POINTS** value: *1.*

*See In the Kitchen p. 154

# Summertime Blueberry Pie

prep 15 min   cook 5 min   serves 8

2   tablespoons cornstarch

2   tablespoons water

3   pints blueberries

½   cup sugar

1   (6-ounce) prepared reduced-fat graham cracker crust

1 Whisk together the cornstarch and water in a large saucepan until smooth. Add 3 cups of the blueberries and the sugar. Bring to a boil over medium-high heat, stirring frequently and pressing the blueberries against the side of the saucepan with a wooden spoon to crush them. Cook, stirring constantly, until the mixture thickens and boils, about 1 minute.

2 Remove the saucepan from the heat and stir in the remaining blueberries. Pour the filling into the prepared crust. Refrigerate until the filling is set, at least 5 hours or up to overnight. Cut into wedges.

**PER SERVING** (⅛ of pie): 215 Cal, 3 g Fat, 1 g Sat Fat, 0 g Trans Fat, 0 mg Chol, 96 mg Sod, 47 g Carb, 3 g Fib, 2 g Prot, 9 mg Calc. **POINTS** value: **4.**

## In the Kitchen

During the summer when fresh berries are plentiful, at their flavorful best, and reasonably priced, replace 2 cups of the uncooked blueberries with 2 cups of raspberries.

**SUMMERTIME BLUEBERRY PIE**

# Caramel-Banana Pie

prep 20 min   microwave 10 min   serves 10

¼  cup pecans, toasted and
    chopped

1   (6-ounce) prepared chocolate
    cookie crust

3   bananas, sliced

1   (3-ounce) box butterscotch
    pudding mix (not instant)

2   cups low-fat (1%) milk

1   cup thawed frozen fat-free
    whipped topping

½  cup caramel or butterscotch
    fat-free ice cream topping

1 Sprinkle 2 tablespoons of the pecans over the bottom of the crust. Arrange the banana slices on top of the pecans in two layers.

2 Whisk together the pudding mix and milk in a large microwavable bowl until blended. Microwave on High 3 minutes; stir. Microwave until the pudding thickens and comes to a full boil, about 4 minutes longer, stirring after every minute of cooking time. Pour the pudding over the bananas and smooth the top. Refrigerate until well chilled, at least 4 hours or up to overnight.

3 To serve, spread the whipped topping over the filling and sprinkle with the remaining 2 tablespoons pecans. Cut the pie into wedges and drizzle evenly with the caramel topping.

PER SERVING (1/10 of pie): 232 Cal, 8 g Fat, 2 g Sat Fat, 0 g Trans Fat, 5 mg Chol, 217 mg Sod, 39 g Carb, 2 g Fib, 3 g Prot, 76 mg Calc. **POINTS** value: **5.**

## In the Kitchen

Toasting the pecans serves two purposes: it crisps the nuts and it brings out their buttery flavor.

# Strawberry Cream Tart

prep 25 min   bake/microwave 15 min   serves 8

¼   cup sliced almonds, chopped

3   tablespoons granulated sugar

Pinch cinnamon

10   (9 x 14-inch) sheets frozen phyllo dough, thawed

1   cup fat-free Greek yogurt

2   tablespoons packed brown sugar

1½ (1-pound) containers strawberries, hulled and quartered

¼   cup strawberry jam

1 Preheat the oven to 350°F. Spray a 9-inch removable bottom tart pan with nonstick spray.

2 Mix together the almonds, 2 tablespoons of the granulated sugar, and the cinnamon in a small bowl. Stack 2 phyllo sheets and place in the prepared pan. Cover the remaining phyllo with a damp paper towel and plastic wrap to keep it from drying out. Gently press the phyllo against the sides and bottom of the pan, allowing it to extend over the rim of the pan. Spray with nonstick spray and sprinkle with 1 tablespoon of the almond-sugar mixture. Repeat 4 more times, placing each new pair of phyllo sheets slightly off center, so the entire pan is covered.

3 Roll in the overhanging phyllo to form a ¾-inch-high edge; spray with nonstick spray. Bake until browned, about 15 minutes. Let cool completely on a wire rack, pressing the phyllo down in the center if puffed.

4 Mix together the yogurt and brown sugar in a small bowl. Toss the strawberries with the remaining 1 tablespoon granulated sugar in a medium bowl. Heat the jam in a small microwavable bowl on High until warm.

5 Remove the pan sides and place the tart on a serving plate. Spoon the yogurt mixture into the tart shell and spread evenly. Spoon the strawberries over the yogurt and drizzle with the jam. Cut into wedges and serve at once.

PER SERVING (⅛ of tart): 149 Cal, 2 g Fat, 0 g Sat Fat, 0 g Trans Fat, 1 mg Chol, 74 mg Sod, 30 g Carb, 2 g Fib, 4 g Prot, 86 mg Calc. **POINTS** value: **3.**

**FROSTED CARROT CAKE CUPCAKES**

# Frosted Carrot Cake Cupcakes

prep 25 min   bake 20 min   makes 2 dozen

1   (18¼-ounce) box spice cake mix
¾   cup fat-free egg substitute
½   cup applesauce
½   cup fat-free buttermilk
2   cups shredded carrots
1   (8-ounce) can crushed pineapple in juice, drained
¼   cup dried currants
½   cup pecans, chopped
4   ounces light cream cheese (Neufchâtel)
1½  cups confectioners' sugar

1 Preheat the oven to 350°F. Line 24 muffin cups with paper liners.

2 With an electric mixer on low speed, beat the cake mix, egg substitute, applesauce, and buttermilk in a large bowl until blended. Increase the speed to medium and beat until smooth, about 2 minutes. With a rubber spatula, stir in the carrots, pineapple, currants, and ¼ cup of the pecans.

3 Spoon the batter evenly into the prepared muffin cups. Bake until a toothpick inserted into the center of a cupcake comes out clean, about 20 minutes. Let cool in the pans on wire racks 10 minutes; remove the cupcakes from the pans and let cool on the racks.

4 To make the frosting, with an electric mixer on low speed, beat the cream cheese in a medium bowl until smooth. Add the confectioners' sugar and beat until smooth. Spread about 2 teaspoons of the frosting on each cupcake and sprinkle with ½ teaspoon of the remaining pecans.

PER SERVING (1 cupcake): 167 Cal, 5 g Fat, 1 g Sat Fat, 0 g Trans Fat, 4 mg Chol, 193 mg Sod, 29 g Carb, 1 g Fib, 3 g Prot, 54 mg Calc. **POINTS** value: **4.**

## In the Kitchen
If you have only one muffin pan, bake the cupcakes in two batches. And if you prefer your cupcakes unfrosted, simply dust them with confectioners' sugar when cool.

# Blueberry-Orange Mini–Tea Breads

prep 15 min   bake 30 min   serves 16

1    cup all-purpose flour
1    cup white whole-wheat flour*
²/₃   cup sugar
2    tablespoons cornmeal
1¹/₂ teaspoons baking powder
¹/₂   teaspoon baking soda
¹/₂   teaspoon salt
2    teaspoons grated orange zest
1    cup orange juice
3    tablespoons canola oil
1    large egg
1¹/₂ cups blueberries

1 Preheat the oven to 350°F. Spray four 5³/₄ x 3¹/₂ x 2-inch disposable loaf pans with nonstick spray.

2 Whisk together the all-purpose flour, white whole-wheat flour, sugar, cornmeal, baking powder, baking soda, and salt in a large bowl. Whisk together the orange zest and juice, oil, and egg in a medium bowl. Add the orange juice mixture to the flour mixture, stirring just until moistened. Gently stir in the blueberries.

3 Spoon the batter evenly into the prepared pans. Bake until a toothpick inserted into the center of a loaf comes out clean, about 30 minutes. Let cool in the pans on a wire rack 10 minutes. Turn the loaves out onto the rack and let cool completely. Cut each loaf into 8 slices.

PER SERVING (2 slices): 134 Cal, 3 g Fat, 0 g Sat Fat, 0 g Trans Fat, 13 mg Chol, 164 mg Sod, 25 g Carb, 2 g Fib, 3 g Prot, 33 mg Calc. **POINTS** value: **3.**

*See In the Kitchen p. 154

# No-Bake Cannoli Cheesecake

prep 25 min   microwave 1 min   serves 12

16   amaretti cookies, coarsely crushed

¼   cup whole unblanched almonds, toasted and chopped

1   envelope unflavored gelatin

⅓   cup cold water

1   (8-ounce) package fat-free cream cheese

1   (15-ounce) container part-skim ricotta cheese

½   cup sugar

⅓   cup fat-free Greek yogurt

1   teaspoon grated orange zest

1   teaspoon vanilla extract

1   cup thawed frozen fat-free whipped topping

⅓   cup mini semisweet chocolate chips

1 Spray a 9-inch springform pan with nonstick spray.

2 Mix together the cookies and almonds in a small bowl. Reserve 2 tablespoons of the mixture. Sprinkle the remaining cookie mixture over the bottom of the prepared pan.

3 Sprinkle the gelatin over the water in a small microwavable bowl; let stand 5 minutes. Microwave on High 45 seconds, stirring until the gelatin is dissolved.

4 With an electric mixer on medium speed, beat the cream cheese in a large bowl until smooth. Add the ricotta, sugar, yogurt, orange zest, and vanilla, beating until blended. Beat in the gelatin. Refrigerate the mixture until it begins to mound, about 20 minutes, stirring occasionally. Fold in the whipped topping and chocolate chips. Spoon over the cookie mixture and smooth the top. Refrigerate until set, at least 5 hours or up to overnight. Sprinkle with the reserved 2 tablespoons cookie mixture.

PER SERVING (1/12 of cake): 191 Cal, 7 g Fat, 3 g Sat Fat, 0 g Trans Fat, 13 mg Chol, 159 mg Sod, 24 g Carb, 1 g Fib, 9 g Prot, 156 mg Calc. **POINTS** value: **4.**

# Baby Plum Cakes

prep 20 min   bake 30 min   serves 6

1 cup all-purpose flour
1/4 teaspoon baking powder
1/4 teaspoon baking soda
1/4 teaspoon salt
3 tablespoons unsalted butter, softened
1/2 cup + 2 tablespoons sugar
1 large egg
1/2 teaspoon vanilla extract
1/3 cup light sour cream
3 red or purple plums, halved and pitted
1/4 teaspoon cinnamon
Sifted confectioners' sugar (optional)

1 Preheat the oven to 350°F. Spray a 6-cup jumbo nonstick muffin pan with nonstick spray or line with paper liners.

2 Whisk together the flour, baking powder, baking soda, and salt in a small bowl. With an electric mixer on medium speed, beat the butter in a medium bowl until creamy. Gradually beat in 1/2 cup of the sugar; beat until fluffy, about 3 minutes. Beat in the egg and vanilla. Reduce the mixer speed to low. Beat in the flour mixture alternately with the sour cream, beginning and ending with the flour mixture, beating just until blended.

3 Spoon the batter evenly into the prepared muffin cups. Place a plum half, cut side up, in each cup, pressing it slightly into the batter.

4 Mix together the remaining 2 tablespoons sugar and the cinnamon. Sprinkle evenly over the plums. Bake until a toothpick inserted into a cake comes out clean, about 25 minutes. Let the cakes cool completely in the pan on a wire rack. To remove the cakes, run a small knife around the sides of each cake to loosen it, then sprinkle lightly with confectioners' sugar if using.

PER SERVING (1 cake): 255 Cal, 9 g Fat, 5 g Sat Fat, 0 g Trans Fat, 56 mg Chol, 188 mg Sod, 41 g Carb, 1 g Fib, 4 g Prot, 37 mg Calc. *POINTS* value: **6.**

## In the Kitchen

These tender little cakes also work well with halved and pitted large apricots, or small peaches or nectarines.

**BABY PLUM CAKES**

*Chocolate*

*Chocolate*

*Chocolate*

chapter 5

# Watermelon with Bittersweet Chocolate Shavings

prep 10 min   cook none   serves 4

| | |
|---|---|
| 4 | cups ³/₄-inch chunks cold seedless watermelon |
| ½ | teaspoon grated orange zest |
| 2 | tablespoons orange juice |
| 1 | tablespoon sugar |
| ½ | ounce bittersweet chocolate |

Toss together the watermelon, orange zest and juice, and sugar in a medium bowl. Spoon the watermelon and any juice evenly into 4 dessert dishes. With a vegetable peeler, shave the chocolate evenly on top.

PER SERVING (1 cup): 79 Cal, 2 g Fat, 1 g Sat Fat, 0 g Trans Fat, 0 mg Chol, 2 mg Sod, 17 g Carb, 1 g Fib, 1 g Prot, 13 mg Calc. **POINTS** value: **2.**

## In the Kitchen

Making neat chocolate shavings is easiest if you hold the chocolate in your hand for a few seconds to allow the warmth of your hand to soften the chocolate slightly.

# Frozen Hot Chocolate

prep 15 min   cook 5 min   serves 4

- 1½ cups fat-free milk
- ¼ cup sugar
- 3 tablespoons unsweetened Dutch-process cocoa
- 2 ounces semisweet chocolate, chopped
- 3 cups ice cubes

1 Combine ½ cup of the milk, the sugar, and cocoa in a medium saucepan and set over medium-low heat. Cook, whisking constantly, until the mixture comes to a boil, about 5 minutes. Remove the saucepan from the heat and stir in the chocolate. Let stand 5 minutes, then stir until the chocolate is melted and the mixture is smooth. Refrigerate until cold, about 20 minutes.

2 Combine the remaining 1 cup milk, the chocolate mixture, and the ice cubes in a blender; blend on high speed until slushy. Pour evenly into 4 glasses or goblets. Serve at once with spoons.

**PER SERVING** (1 cup): 157 Cal, 5 g Fat, 2 g Sat Fat, 0 g Trans Fat, 2 mg Chol, 41 mg Sod, 33 g Carb, 3 g Fib, 5 g Prot, 121 mg Calc. **POINTS** value: **3.**

## So Satisfying
Thick and super slushy, this refresher is sure to hit the spot on the hottest of days. Prepare a double—or triple—batch of the cocoa mixture and store in a covered container in the refrigerator up to 3 days so it's ready to go.

# Double Chocolate Brownie Smash

prep 5 min   cook none   serves 2

1   **cup ice cubes**

2   **tablespoons fat-free milk**

2   **tablespoons light chocolate syrup**

½   **cup chocolate fat-free frozen yogurt, slightly softened**

1   **(1½-ounce) fat-free brownie, diced**

Combine the ice cubes, milk, and chocolate syrup in a blender and blend until slushy. Pour evenly into 2 glasses. Lightly stir in the frozen yogurt and brownie pieces. Serve at once with spoons or straws.

PER SERVING (¾ cup): 158 Cal, 0 g Fat, 0 g Sat Fat, 0 g Trans Fat, 1 mg Chol, 153 mg Sod, 35 g Carb, 1 g Fib, 4 g Prot, 119 mg Calc. *POINTS* value: **3.**

## So Satisfying

This spoonable shake has it all. It's cool, it's creamy, it's icy and, best of all, it's packed with lots of rich chocolate flavor. And all it takes is 5 quick minutes to prepare.

**DOUBLE CHOCOLATE BROWNIE SMASH**

# Deep Chocolate Mousse

prep 15 min   microwave 1 min   serves 6

| | |
|---|---|
| 3 | ounces bittersweet or semisweet chocolate, chopped |
| ¼ | cup fat-free half-and-half |
| ¼ | cup unsweetened cocoa |
| ¼ | cup confectioners' sugar |
| 1 | (6-ounce) container vanilla low-fat yogurt |
| 1 | cup thawed frozen fat-free whipped topping |

1 Combine the chocolate and half-and-half in a medium microwavable bowl. Microwave on High 1 minute. Let stand 1 minute, then whisk until the chocolate is melted and smooth. Let cool 10 minutes.

2 Strain the cocoa and confectioners' sugar through a sieve set over the chocolate mixture. Whisk the mixture until smooth, then add the yogurt, whisking until blended. Gently fold in the whipped topping just until no white streaks remain. Spoon the mousse evenly into 6 dessert dishes. Refrigerate up to 8 hours.

PER SERVING (about ⅓ cup): 147 Cal, 7 g Fat, 4 g Sat Fat, 0 g Trans Fat, 2 mg Chol, 39 mg Sod, 23 g Carb, 2 g Fib, 3 g Prot, 70 mg Calc. **POINTS** value: **3.**

◆ Filling Extra
Top each serving with ¼ cup raspberries or sliced strawberries.

# Super S'mores

prep 10 min   broil 1 min   serves 4

**2**   whole reduced-fat graham crackers

**1**   (1½-ounce) milk chocolate bar, broken into 4 pieces

**1**   cup chocolate fat-free frozen yogurt

**1**   cup miniature marshmallows

1 Preheat the broiler.

2 Break each graham cracker in half. Place the graham cracker squares on a small baking sheet in one layer. Top each square with 1 piece of chocolate.

3 Broil 5 inches from the heat until the chocolate softens, about 30 seconds. Top each with a ¼-cup scoop of frozen yogurt. Working quickly and starting at the top of the yogurt, press the marshmallows into the frozen yogurt to cover. Broil until the marshmallows are browned, about 30 seconds. Serve at once.

PER SERVING (1 s'more): 181 Cal, 1 g Fat, 2 g Sat Fat, 0 g Trans Fat, 4 mg Chol, 87 mg Sod, 34 g Carb, 1 g Fib, 4 g Prot, 107 mg Calc. **POINTS** value: **4.**

**MILK CHOCOLATE AND HAZELNUT TOASTED SANDWICHES**

# Milk Chocolate and Hazelnut Toasted Sandwiches

prep 10 min   cook 4 min   serves 4

2   tablespoons milk chocolate–
    hazelnut spread (Nutella)

4   slices whole-grain sandwich
    bread

1   ounce semisweet or bittersweet
    chocolate, chopped

1 Spread 1 tablespoon of the milk-chocolate-and-hazelnut spread on each of 2 slices of the bread. Sprinkle evenly with the chocolate and cover with the remaining slices of bread, lightly pressing down.

2 Place the sandwiches in a dry large nonstick skillet and set over medium-low heat. Cook until browned, about 3 minutes. Turn and cook until browned, about 2 minutes longer. Transfer the sandwiches to a cutting board and let stand 5 minutes. Cut each in half or into quarters.

PER SERVING (1/2 panini): 154 Cal, 6 g Fat, 2 g Sat Fat, 0 g Trans Fat, 0 mg Chol, 138 mg Sod, 22 g Carb, 3 g Fib, 4 g Prot, 43 mg Calc. **POINTS** value: **3.**

## So Satisfying

Nutella, an oh-so-creamy milk chocolate and hazelnut spread, is found alongside the peanut butter in supermarkets. These panini, crisp on the outside and all melty on the inside, are the perfect mid-afternoon pick-me-up.

# Black and White Muffin Bites

prep 10 min  bake 10 min  serves 18

| | |
|---|---|
| 1 | cup all-purpose flour |
| ½ | cup sugar |
| ⅓ | cup unsweetened cocoa |
| 1 | teaspoon baking soda |
| ¼ | teaspoon salt |
| ½ | cup fat-free milk |
| 3 | tablespoons canola oil |
| 1 | large egg |
| 1 | large egg white |
| 1 | teaspoon vanilla extract |
| ¾ | cup white chocolate chips |

1 Preheat the oven to 350°F. Line 36 mini-muffin cups with paper liners.

2 Whisk the flour, sugar, cocoa, baking soda, and salt in a large bowl. Whisk together the milk, oil, egg, egg white, and vanilla in a small bowl. Add the milk mixture and ½ cup of the chocolate chips to the flour mixture , stirring just until moistened. Spoon the batter evenly into the prepared muffin cups, filling each about halfway.

3 Sprinkle the remaining ¼ cup chocolate chips evenly over the tops of the muffins. Bake until the muffins spring back when lightly pressed, about 10 minutes. Let the muffins cool in the pans on wire racks 10 minutes. Remove the muffins from the pans and let cool completely on the racks.

**PER SERVING** (2 mini muffin s): 116 Cal, 6 g Fat, 2 g Sat Fat, 0 g Trans Fat, 14 mg Chol, 118 mg Sod, 16 g Carb, 0 g Fib, 2 g Prot, 28 mg Calc. **POINTS** value: **3.**

# Crunchy Chocolate-Almond Cereal Squares

prep 15 min   cook 5 min   serves 24

3   cups air-popped plain popcorn
2   cups crispy rice cereal
2   cups oat circle cereal
3/4 cup whole unblanched almonds, toasted
2   tablespoons butter
1   ounce unsweetened chocolate, chopped
1   (7 ½-ounce) jar marshmallow crème
3   tablespoons unsweetened cocoa
2   teaspoons vanilla extract

1 Line a 9 x 13-inch baking pan with foil, allowing the excess foil to extend over the rim of the pan by 2 inches. Spray with nonstick spray.

2 Mix together the popcorn, rice cereal, and oat cereal in a very large bowl. Put the almonds in a food processor and process until chopped. Stir 1/3 cup of the nuts into the cereal mixture. Process the remaining almonds until a smooth nut butter forms, about 2 minutes.

3 Put the butter and chocolate in a large nonstick skillet and set over low heat. Cook, stirring, until melted, about 2 minutes. Remove the skillet from the heat; add the marshmallow crème, cocoa, vanilla, and almond butter. Return the skillet to the heat and cook, stirring, until well blended and heated through, about 3 minutes longer.

4 Scrape the marshmallow mixture over the cereal mixture and stir vigorously until the cereal mixture is coated evenly. Turn the mixture into the prepared pan. Lightly spray your hands with nonstick spray and press firmly on the cereal mixture to make an even layer. Let cool completely. Lift the cereal mixture from the pan using the foil as handles. Using a serrated knife, cut into 24 squares.

PER SERVING (1 square): 89 Cal, 4 g Fat, 1 g Sat Fat, 0 g Trans Fat, 3 mg Chol, 30 mg Sod, 12 g Carb, 1 g Fib, 2 g Prot, 24 mg Calc. **POINTS** value: **2.**

## In the Kitchen

There are two kinds of cocoa: natural unsweetened and Dutch-process. Natural cocoa has full, rich chocolate flavor and is the type used most often in baking. (Hershey brand cocoa is natural cocoa.) Dutch-process cocoa has been treated with an alkali, which mellows its flavor and gives baked goods a very deep color.

# Chocolate Cream Stacks

prep 15 min   cook none   serves 4

2   (4-ounce) refrigerated chocolate fat-free pudding snacks

½   teaspoon grated orange zest + additional for garnish

⅓   cup + 3 tablespoons thawed frozen fat-free whipped topping

16   chocolate wafer cookies

1 Stir together the chocolate pudding and orange zest in a medium bowl. Fold in 1/3 cup of the whipped topping.

2 Spread 1 tablespoon of the pudding mixture on each of the cookies. Stack 4 cookies and place on a dessert plate. Repeat to make a total of 4 stacks. Cover loosely with plastic wrap and refrigerate until the cookies soften, at least 4 hours or up to overnight. Top each stack with a dollop of the remaining whipped topping and sprinkle with the remaining orange zest. Serve at once.

PER SERVING (1 stack): 176 Cal, 4 g Fat, 1 g Sat Fat, 0 g Trans Fat, 5 mg Chol, 249 mg Sod, 34 g Carb, 1 g Fib, 3 g Prot, 32 mg Calc. **POINTS** value: **4.**

## So Satisfying
This treat is reminiscent of the time-honored back-of-the-box recipe for the chocolate-wafer-cookies-and-cream cake. Ours is updated and brightened with freshly grated orange zest and turned into fun-to-eat stacks.

**CHOCOLATE CREAM STACKS**

# Chocolate Dipped Fruit

prep 25 min  cook 10 min  serves 12

| | |
|---|---|
| 4 | ounces bittersweet or semisweet chocolate, coarsely chopped |
| 1 | tablespoon vegetable shortening |
| 4 | ounces white chocolate, coarsely chopped |
| 6 | ounces green or red grapes, on the stem |
| 1 | kiwifruit, peeled and cut into 6 slices |
| 12 | unhulled large strawberries |
| 1 | small tangerine or orange, peeled and sectioned |
| 6 | dried apricot halves |
| 3 | dried peach or pear halves, quartered |

1 Bring 1 inch of water to a simmer in a small saucepan. Combine the bittersweet chocolate and 1½ teaspoons of the shortening in a small bowl. Set over the simmering water and cook, stirring, until melted and smooth, about 4 minutes. Remove the bowl from the pan. Repeat with the white chocolate and the remaining 1½ teaspoons vegetable shortening.

2 Line a baking sheet with wax paper. With kitchen scissors, cut the grapes into small clusters. Pat the kiwi slices dry with paper towels. Dip the fresh and dried fruit halfway into one of the chocolate mixtures, one piece at a time, allowing the excess to drip off. Place each dipped piece of fruit on the prepared baking sheet. Refrigerate until the chocolate is set, about 30 minutes.

PER SERVING (¹/₁₂ of fruit): 144 Cal, 8 g Fat, 4 g Sat Fat, 0 g Trans Fat, 2 mg Chol, 11 mg Sod, 20 g Carb, 2 g Fib, 2 g Prot, 34 mg Calc. **POINTS** value: **3**

## In the Kitchen
The fruits can be dipped up to 2 days ahead. Once the chocolate is set, layer the fruit between sheets of wax paper in an airtight container and refrigerate up to 2 days.

# Miniature Whoopie Pies

prep 30 min   bake 15 min   makes 2 dozen

1    **cup white whole-wheat flour\***
¹/₂   **cup sugar**
¹/₄   **cup unsweetened cocoa**
¹/₂   **teaspoon baking soda**
¹/₄   **teaspoon salt**
¹/₃   **cup fat-free milk**
3    **tablespoons canola oil**
1    **large egg white**
1    **teaspoon vanilla extract**
³/₄   **cup marshmallow crème**
2    **tablespoons mini semisweet chocolate chips**

1 Preheat the oven to 350°F. Spray 2 large baking sheets with nonstick spray.

2 Sift the flour, sugar, cocoa, baking soda, and salt into a large bowl. Whisk together the milk, oil, egg white, and vanilla in a small bowl. Add the milk mixture to the flour mixture, stirring until blended. Drop slightly rounded measuring teaspoonfuls of the dough 2 inches apart onto the prepared baking sheets to make a total of 48 cookies.

3 Bake one sheet of cookies at a time until the tops of the cookies spring back when pressed lightly, about 8 minutes. Transfer the cookies to wire racks and let cool completely.

4 Spread 1¹/₂ teaspoons of the marshmallow crème on the bottom of each of 24 of the cookies. Sprinkle each with ¹/₄ teaspoon mini chips. Cover each with another cookie, bottom side down, and lightly press together. Layer the cookies between sheets of waxed paper in an airtight container and refrigerate up to 3 days.

**PER SERVING** (1 cookie): 67 Cal, 2 g Fat, 0 g Sat Fat, 0 g Trans Fat, 0 mg Chol, 58 mg Sod, 12 g Carb, 1 g Fib, 1 g Prot, 8 mg Calc. ***POINTS*** value: *1.*

## In the Kitchen
These Pennsylvania-Dutch favorites are not pies at all but rather two cakelike cookies that are sandwiched together with a marshmallow crème filling. They are also sometimes called moon pies, presumably because they are often rather large.

\*See In the Kitchen p. 154

# Slice and Bake Chocolate Cookies

prep 25 min   bake 10 min   makes 42

¼   cup old-fashioned (rolled) oats

1   cup all-purpose flour

½   cup unsweetened Dutch-process cocoa

¼   teaspoon baking soda

¼   teaspoon salt

4   tablespoons light stick butter, softened

½   cup granulated sugar

½   cup packed brown sugar

1   large egg white

1½ teaspoons vanilla extract

1 Put the oats in a blender and blend until finely ground.

2 Sift the flour, cocoa, baking soda, and salt into a small bowl; stir in the ground oats.

3 With an electric mixer on medium speed, beat the butter, granulated sugar, and brown sugar in a large bowl until creamy. Beat in the egg white and vanilla. Reduce the mixer speed to low and beat in the flour mixture just until blended. Refrigerate the dough about 15 minutes.

4 Shape the dough into an 11-inch log and wrap tightly in plastic wrap. Refrigerate until firm, at least 2 hours or up to 4 days.

5 Preheat the oven to 350°F. Spray 2 large baking sheets with nonstick spray.

6 Cut the log into scant ¼-inch slices and arrange 2 inches apart on the prepared baking sheets. Bake until the cookies puff then fall, about 10 minutes. With a spatula, transfer the cookies to wire racks and let cool.

PER SERVING (2 cookies): 80 Cal, 1 g Fat, 1 g Sat Fat, 0 g Trans Fat, 3 mg Chol, 62 mg Sod, 16 g Carb, 1 g Fib, 1 g Prot, 8 mg Calc. **POINTS** value: **1.**

# Very Chocolate Rice Pudding

prep 15 min   cook/microwave 35 min   serves 4

1  cup water

½  cup instant brown rice

2  cups low-fat (1%) milk

⅓  cup sugar

¼  cup unsweetened cocoa, preferably Dutch-process

3  tablespoons cornstarch

Pinch salt

¼  cup semisweet chocolate chips

1  teaspoon vanilla extract

1 Combine the water and rice in a medium saucepan and bring to a boil over high heat. Reduce the heat to low and simmer, covered, until the water is absorbed and the rice is very tender, about 20 minutes. Transfer to a small bowl.

2 Pour 1½ cups of the milk into a 2-cup glass measure. Microwave on High until hot, about 2 minutes.

3 Whisk together the sugar, cocoa, cornstarch, and salt in a clean medium saucepan until blended. Whisk in the remaining ½ cup cold milk until combined well; whisk in the hot milk.

4 Cook the milk mixture over medium heat, stirring constantly with a silicone (heatproof) spatula until the pudding bubbles and thickens, about 6 minutes. Reduce the heat to low and stir in the rice. Cook, stirring, 2 minutes. Add the chocolate and stir until melted and smooth.

5 Remove the saucepan from the heat and stir in the vanilla. Divide the pudding evenly among into 4 dessert dishes. Serve warm or cover each dish with a piece of plastic wrap and refrigerate until cold, about 4 hours.

PER SERVING (⅔ cup): 249 Cal, 5 g Fat, 3 Sat Fat, 0 g Trans Fat, 6 mg Chol, 132 mg Sod, 47 g Carb, 4 g Fib, 7 g Prot, 162 mg Calc. **POINTS** value: **5.**

◆ Filling Extra

We've replaced the usual white rice typically used in rice puddings with quick-cooking brown rice, which lends an appealing slightly chewy texture—a good contrast to the creamy pudding. Top each serving with ½ cup sliced strawberries.

**EASY CHOCOLATE SKILLET SOUFFLÉ**

# Easy Chocolate Skillet Soufflé

prep 15 min   microwave/bake 15 min   serves 10

⅓ cup + 2 tablespoons sugar

7 ounces good-quality semisweet chocolate, chopped

¼ cup fat-free milk

2 large eggs, separated

2 large egg whites

Pinch salt

10 tablespoons thawed frozen fat-free whipped topping (optional)

1 Preheat the oven to 400°F. Spray a 10-inch ovenproof skillet with nonstick spray and sprinkle evenly with 2 tablespoons of the sugar.

2 Combine the chocolate and milk in a large microwavable bowl. Microwave on high 1 minute. Whisk until the chocolate is melted and the mixture is smooth. Whisk in the egg yolks.

3 With an electric mixer on medium speed, beat the 4 egg whites and salt in a medium bowl until soft peaks form. Increase the speed to medium-high. Add the remaining ⅓ cup sugar, 1 tablespoon at a time, beating just until stiff peaks form. Fold one-fourth of the whites into the chocolate mixture. Gently fold in the remaining whites just until no white streaks remain.

4 Gently pour the chocolate mixture into the prepared skillet. Bake until the soufflé springs back when lightly pressed in the center, 12–15 minutes.

5 Serve at once accompanied by whipped topping if using. Leftovers can be gently warmed in the microwave on Medium-low power.

PER SERVING (½ cup soufflé without whipped cream): 151 Cal, 7 g Fat, 4 g Sat Fat, 0 g Trans Fat, 43 mg Chol, 57 mg Sod, 22 g Carb, 1 g Fib, 3 g Prot, 20 mg Calc. **POINTS** value: **3.**

## In the Kitchen

Baking this soufflé in a skillet rather than in a soufflé dish makes it more casual and it requires less baking time. The texture of this very chocolaty soufflé is like that of the creamiest and lightest chocolate cake you've ever tasted.

# Chocolate-Raspberry Sorbet Sandwiches

prep 5 min   cook none   serves 2

| | |
|---|---|
| ¼ | cup chocolate sorbet, slightly softened |
| 4 | ½-inch slices fat-free pound cake |
| ¼ | cup raspberry sorbet, slightly softened |

Spread 2 tablespoons of the chocolate sorbet on each of 2 slices of the pound cake. Spread 2 tablespoons of the raspberry sorbet on each of the remaining 2 slices. Place a raspberry sorbet topped cake slice on top of each chocolate sorbet topped cake slice, sorbet sides facing each other. Serve at once or wrap in plastic wrap and freeze up to 2 days.

PER SERVING (1 sandwich): 279 Cal, 0 g Fat, 0 g Sat Fat, 0 g Trans Fat, 0 mg Chol, 257 mg Sod, 68 g Carb, 2 g Fib, 4 g Prot, 145 mg Calc. **POINTS** value: **5.**

## In the Kitchen
Substitute any combination of sorbet flavors that strikes your fancy, such as lemon and blueberry, mango and raspberry, or mixed berry and passion fruit.

# Rocky Road Ice Cream Cake

prep 25 min   cook none   serves 16

16 reduced-fat chocolate sandwich cookies, crushed

1 pint chocolate fat-free frozen yogurt, slightly softened

1 pint vanilla fat-free frozen yogurt, slightly softened

1 pint coffee fat-free ice cream, slightly softened

1/2 cup miniature marshmallows

1/4 cup salted cocktail peanuts

1/2 cup fat-free hot fudge sauce, heated

1 Reserve 2 tablespoons of the crushed cookies. Sprinkle the remaining crumbs evenly over the bottom of a 9-inch springform pan.

2 Spoon the chocolate frozen yogurt over the cookie crumbs, spreading it to form an even layer. Freeze until firm, about 20 minutes. Repeat with the vanilla frozen yogurt and then the coffee ice cream. Wrap the pan tightly in foil and freeze until completely frozen, at least 6 hours or up to 1 week.

3 Remove the foil from the pan. Sprinkle the marshmallows, peanuts, and reserved crushed cookies evenly over the coffee ice cream, pressing lightly so they adhere.

4 Run a knife around the sides of the cake; remove the pan sides. Using a large knife, cut the cake Into wedges, rinsing the knife under hot water between cuts and shaking off the excess water. Drizzle evenly with the fudge sauce and serve at once.

PER SERVING (1/16 of cake and 1 1/2 teaspoons sauce): 163 Cal, 3 g Fat, 1 g Sat Fat, 0 g Trans Fat, 1 mg Chol, 140 mg Sod, 32 g Carb, 1 g Fib, 4 g Prot, 115 mg Calc. *POINTS* value: **3.**

## In the Kitchen

This dessert is so easy to put together yet impressive enough to serve for a special dinner or celebration party. You can substitute any combination of yogurt and ice cream flavors you like to personalize it.

# Chocolate Hazelnut Semifreddo

prep 15 min   cook none   serves 16

1   (5.9-ounce) box instant
    chocolate pudding and pie filling
¼   cup unsweetened cocoa,
    preferably Dutch-process
3   cups low-fat (1%) milk
2½  cups thawed frozen fat-free
    whipped topping
½   cup hazelnuts, toasted, skinned,
    and chopped
1   ounce bittersweet chocolate,
    finely chopped
½   cup light chocolate syrup

1 Line a 5 x 9-inch loaf pan with plastic wrap, allowing the excess foil to extend over the ends of the pan by 5 inches.

2 Whisk together the chocolate pudding and cocoa in a large bowl. Add the milk and whisk until thoroughly blended, about 2 minutes; let stand 5 minutes. Fold in the whipped topping, hazelnuts, and bittersweet chocolate until blended. Scrape the mixture into the prepared pan, smoothing the top. Wrap the pan in heavy foil and freeze until firm, at least 6 hours or up to 4 days.

3 Let the semifreddo soften at room temperature about 20 minutes. Remove the foil and invert the loaf pan onto a cutting board. Remove the pan and plastic wrap. With a long, serrated knife, cut the loaf into 16 (1/2-inch) slices. Place the slices on plates and drizzle evenly with the chocolate syrup.

PER SERVING (1/16 of cake and 1/2 tablespoon syrup): 126 Cal, 4 g Fat, 1 g Sat Fat, 0 g Trans Fat, 2 mg Chol, 182 mg Sod, 21 g Carb, 1 g Fib, 3 g Prot, 65 mg Calc. **POINTS** value: **3.**

## In the Kitchen
*Semifreddo* is Italian for half-cold, which perfectly describes the texture of this temptingly creamy, partially frozen dessert. We recommend letting it stand at room temperature for about 20 minutes before slicing, or until the edges become creamy and soft, while the center remains nicely semi-frozen.

# Creamy Chocolate Walnut Fudge

prep 10 min   cook 5 min   makes 4 dozen

14  ounces semisweet chocolate,
    chopped

2   ounces unsweetened chocolate,
    chopped

1   (14-ounce) can fat-free
    sweetened condensed milk

3/4  cup chopped walnuts

2   teaspoons vanilla extract

Pinch salt

1 Line an 8-inch square baking pan with foil allowing the excess foil to extend over the rim of the pan at two opposite sides by 2 inches. Spray with nonstick spray.

2 Combine the semisweet chocolate, unsweetened chocolate, and condensed milk in a large saucepan and set over low heat. Cook, stirring, until the chocolate is melted and the mixture is smooth, about 5 minutes. Remove the saucepan from the heat; stir in the walnuts, vanilla, and salt.

3 Turn the mixture into the prepared pan and spread evenly. Let cool completely Lift the fudge from the pan using the foil as handles. With a long, thin knife, cut the fudge into 6 strips, then cut each strip crosswise into 8 pieces.

PER SERVING (1 piece fudge): 81 Cal, 4 g Fat, 2 g Sat Fat, 0 g Trans Fat, 0 mg Chol, 15 mg Sod, 11 g Carb, 1 g Fib, 1 g Prot, 29 mg Calc. **POINTS** value: **2.**

## In the Kitchen
Layer the pieces of fudge between sheets of wax paper in an airtight container and refrigerate up to 1 week. Let come to room temperature before serving.

# Triple Chocolate Brownie Thins

prep 10 min  microwave/bake 15 min  serves 12

| | |
|---|---|
| 1 | ounce unsweetened chocolate, chopped |
| 2 | tablespoons butter |
| 3 | tablespoons unsweetened Dutch-process cocoa |
| 1/2 | cup sugar |
| 1 | large egg |
| 1/2 | teaspoon vanilla extract |
| 1/3 | cup all-purpose flour |
| 1/8 | teaspoon baking powder |
| 1/8 | teaspoon salt |
| 1/4 | cup + 2 tablespoons semisweet chocolate chips |

1 Preheat the oven to 350°F. Line a 9-inch round baking pan with foil allowing the excess foil to extend over the rim of the pan by 2 inches. Lightly spray with nonstick spray.

2 Combine the unsweetened chocolate and butter in a medium microwavable bowl. Microwave on High 1 minute, then whisk until smooth. Whisk in the cocoa until blended. Whisk in the sugar, egg, and vanilla. Add the flour, baking powder, and salt; stir just until blended. Stir in 1/4 cup of the chocolate chips.

3 Scrape the batter into the prepared pan, spreading it to cover the bottom of the pan. Sprinkle evenly with the remaining 2 tablespoons chocolate chips. Bake until the brownies are firm along the edges and a toothpick inserted into the center comes out with moist crumbs clinging, 12–14 minutes. Let cool completely in the pan on a wire rack. Remove the brownies from the baking pan using the foil as handles. Cut into 12 wedges.

PER SERVING (1 wedge): 106 Cal, 5 g Fat, 3 g Sat Fat, 0 g Trans Fat, 23 mg Chol, 49 mg Sod, 15 g Carb, 1 g Fib, 2 g Prot, 12 mg Calc. **POINTS** value: **2.**

## So Satisfying

Bite into a slim wedge of this brownie and enjoy deep chocolate flavor three ways: from the unsweetened chocolate, the semisweet chocolate chips, and the cocoa. Serve each brownie with a glass of fat-free milk (1/2 cup fat-free milk for each serving will increase the **POINTS** value by **1**).

**TRIPLE CHOCOLATE BROWNIE THINS**

# Cocoa-Covered Mocha Truffles

prep 20 min   cook 5 min   makes 32

8   ounces good-quality semisweet chocolate, chopped

3   tablespoons unsalted butter

⅓   cup fat-free half-and-half

2   teaspoons instant coffee powder

⅓   cup unsweetened cocoa

1 Combine the chocolate and butter in a medium saucepan and set over low heat. Cook, stirringing, frequently, until melted and smooth; remove the saucepan from the heat. Stir in the half-and-half and coffee powder until blended. Scrape the chocolate mixture into a medium bowl. Cover the bowl with plastic wrap and refrigerate until the chocolate mixture is firm, at least 3 hours or up to 2 days.

2 Put the cocoa powder in a small bowl. Dust your hands with cocoa powder. Divide the truffle mixture into 32 portions. Quickly roll each portion into ball, then roll in the cocoa to coat evenly. Layer the truffles between sheets of wax paper in a covered container. Cover and refrigerate up to 1 week.

PER SERVING (1 truffle): 47 Cal, 3 g Fat, 2 g Sat Fat, 0 g Trans Fat, 3 mg Chol, 5 mg Sod, 5 g Carb, 1 g Fib, 1 g Prot, 6 mg Calc. *POINTS* value: *1.*

## So Satisfying

Super creamy and oh so chocolaty, these truffles are a real delight. Though easy enough to make for an everyday treat, they also make the perfect addition to a dessert tray. If you love truffles with a hint of liqueur, leave out the coffee powder and add 2 tablespoons Grand Marnier, or Tia Maria along with the half-and-half in step 1.

# Chocolate Fudge Truffle Tart

prep 30 min   bake/microwave 10 min   serves 16

---

30   chocolate wafer cookies, halved

5   tablespoons sugar

1   tablespoon butter, melted

1   tablespoon light or dark corn syrup

10   ounces bittersweet chocolate, chopped

1   (14-ounce) can fat-free sweetened condensed milk

1   cup thawed frozen fat-free whipped topping

1   cup fat-free Greek yogurt

2   cups sweet cherries, pitted and quartered

1 Preheat the oven to 350°F.

2 To make the crust, combine the cookies and 1 tablespoon of the sugar in a food processor; process until finely ground. Mix together the butter and corn syrup in a cup. Drizzle over the cookie crumbs and pulse until evenly moistened. Press the mixture onto the bottom and against the sides of a 9-inch removable bottom tart pan. Bake until set, about 8 minutes. Let cool.

3 To make the filling, combine the chocolate and condensed milk in a large microwavable bowl. Microwave on High 1 minute. Stir until the chocolate is melted; microwave an additional 30 seconds, if necessary. Let cool 15 minutes.

4 Fold the whipped topping into the chocolate mixture. Scrape the filling into the tart shell. Refrigerate until firm, at least 4 hours.

5 To serve, stir together the yogurt and 3 tablespoons of the sugar in a small bowl. Toss together the cherries and the remaining 1 tablespoon sugar in a medium bowl. Let stand until the sugar is dissolved. Remove the pan sides and cut the tart into wedges. Place the wedges on plates. Garnish each serving with a dollop of the yogurt mixture and some cherries.

PER SERVING (1/16 of tart, 1 tablespoon yogurt, and 2 tablespoons cherries): 259 Cal, 9 g Fat, 5 g Sat Fat, 0 g Trans Fat, 5 mg Chol, 126 mg Sod, 44 g Carb, 2 g Fib, 5 g Prot, 116 mg Calc. **POINTS** value: **6.**

# Phyllo-Crusted Chocolate-Strawberry Tartlets

prep 25 min   microwave 2 min   serves 24

½   cup confectioners' sugar

2   tablespoons unsweetened cocoa

2   tablespoons fat-free milk

2   ounces bittersweet chocolate, chopped

2   ounces light cream cheese (Neufchâtel), softened

2   tablespoons strawberry jam

24   frozen mini phyllo tart shells, thawed

½   cup thawed frozen fat-free whipped topping

12   small strawberries, hulled and halved

24   small fresh mint sprigs

1 Whisk together the confectioners' sugar, cocoa, and milk in a 2-cup glass measure. Cover with plastic wrap; microwave on High until the mixture comes to a boil, 30 seconds to 1 minute. Add the chocolate and whisk until melted, then add the cream cheese and whisk until smooth. Cover and refrigerate until cold, about 45 minutes.

2 Spread ¼ teaspoon of the jam in the bottom of each tart shell. Top with about 1 teaspoon of the chocolate filling, 1 teaspoon of the whipped topping, and a strawberry half. Garnish each with a mint sprig.

PER SERVING (1 tartlet): 55 Cal, 2 g Fat, 1 g Sat Fat, 0 g Trans Fat, 2 mg Chol, 23 mg Sod, 8 g Carb, 1 g Fib, 1 g Prot, 7 mg Calc. **POINTS** value: **1.**

## So Satisfying

These delicate, delicious little tarts are an explosion of contrasting textures and flavors: crisp phyllo shells, a creamy chocolate filling, and ripe strawberries. Serve them toward the end of a cocktail party as a sweet hors d'oeuvre. Ungarnished, the tarts can be refrigerated up to 6 hours.

# No-Bake Chocolate Cheesecake Bars

prep 15 min   microwave 1 min   serves 12

5   whole chocolate graham crackers

4   ounces semisweet chocolate, chopped

2   (8-ounce) packages fat-free cream cheese, softened

1/3   cup sugar

1   teaspoon vanilla extract

1   cup thawed frozen fat-free whipped topping

1 Line a 9-inch square baking pan with foil, allowing the excess foil to extend over the pan by 2 inches. Spray with nonstick spray. Line the bottom of the pan with the crackers, breaking them to fit, if necessary.

2 Put the chocolate in a microwavable bowl. Microwave on High 45 seconds; stir until melted.

3 With an electric mixer, beat the cream cheese until smooth. Beat in the sugar and vanilla. Fold in the whipped topping. Measure out 1 cup of the cream cheese mixture and reserve. Spoon another 1/4 cup of the cream cheese mixture into a small bowl and reserve. With the mixer, beat three fourths of the melted chocolate into the cheese mixture in the large bowl. Spread evenly into the pan. Spoon the reserved 1 cup cheese mixture over and spread evenly.

4 Stir the remaining melted chocolate into the reserved 1/4 cup cream cheese mixture. Pipe lines of this chocolate mixture, 1 inch apart, over the plain cream cheese mixture in the pan. Draw a table knife through the lines at 1-inch intervals, to create a feathered design. Cover the pan with foil; refrigerate at least 6 hours.

5 To serve, freeze the cheesecake 15 minutes. Remove the cheesecake from the pan. Peel off and discard the foil. Cut the cheesecake into 12 bars, rinsing the knife between cuts.

PER SERVING (1 bar): 136 Cal, 4 g Fat, 2 g Sat Fat, 0 g Trans Fat, 3 mg Chol, 245 mg Sod, 20 g Carb, 1 g Fib, 6 g Prot, 78 mg Calc.
**POINTS** value: **3.**

**ICED MINI–CHOCOLATE LOAVES**

# Iced Mini–Chocolate Loaves

prep 20 min   bake/microwave 30 min   serves 16

1³/₄ cups white whole-wheat flour*

1¹/₄ cups granulated sugar

¹/₂ cup unsweetened cocoa

1 teaspoon baking soda

¹/₂ teaspoon salt

1 cup fat-free buttermilk

1 large egg

2 tablespoons butter, melted

2 tablespoons canola oil

2 teaspoons vanilla extract

1 ounce milk chocolate, chopped

1 tablespoon fat-free half-and-half

¹/₂ cup confectioners' sugar

2 tablespoons salted macadamia nuts, chopped

1 Preheat the oven to 350°F. Spray 4 (5³/₄ x 3¹/₄ x 2-inch) disposable mini–loaf pans with nonstick spray. Dust with flour, shaking out the excess.

2 To make the loaves, whisk together the flour, granulated sugar, cocoa, baking soda, and salt in a large bowl. Whisk together the buttermilk, egg, butter, oil, and vanilla in a medium bowl. Add the buttermilk mixture to the flour mixture, whisking until the batter is blended and smooth.

3 Divide the batter evenly among the prepared pans. Bake until a toothpick inserted into the center of a loaf comes out clean, about 30 minutes. Let cool completely in the pans on a wire rack.

4 To make the icing, combine the milk chocolate and half-and-half in a small microwavable bowl. Microwave on Medium 1 minute. Stir until the chocolate is melted and the mixture is smooth. Add the confectioners' sugar and whisk until smooth. Invert the loaves onto a wire rack. Remove the pans and turn the loaves, right side up. Drizzle the icing over the tops of the loaves and sprinkle evenly with the nuts. Let stand until the icing is set, about 30 minutes.

PER SERVING (2 slices): 185 Cal, 6 g Fat, 2 g Sat Fat, 0 g Trans Fat, 18 mg Chol, 189 mg Sod, 33 g Carb, 3 g Fib, 4 g Prot, 33 mg Calc. **POINTS** value: *4.*

*See In the Kitchen p. 154

# Recipes by *POINTS* value

Cayenne-Spiked Oven-Fried Chicken, 80

Chocolate Cream Stacks, 178

Frosted Carrot Cake Cupcakes, 161

Frozen Key Lime Pie, 148

Garlicky Bean Dip with Sesame Wonton Crisps, 53

Ginger-Lemon Sorbet Sandwiches, 136

Green Chile and Cheese Cornbread, 129

Iced Mini–Chocolate Loaves, 197

Jalapeño and Cilantro–Flavored Codfish Cakes, 86

Light-as-a-Feather Corn Fritters, 67

Marseilles-Style Fish Soup, 43

No-Bake Cannoli Cheesecake, 163

Parmesan and Panko-Crusted Lamb Chops, 77

Roast Chicken Salad with Minted Summer Greens, 38

Rosemary-Rubbed Salmon with Kalamata Olive Topping, 39

Sangria Sorbet, 153

Spice-Rubbed Mango-Glazed Pork Tenderloin, 31

Spiced Lamb with Cooling Yogurt Sauce, 118

Strawberry-Mint Freeze, 150

Streusel-Topped Oven-Roasted Peaches, 141

Summertime Blueberry Pie, 156

Super S'mores, 173

Sweet Berry Focaccia, 147

Turkish-Style Glazed Apricots and Cherries, 137

### 5 POINTS value

Banana Split Ice-Cream Sandwiches, 145

Caramel-Banana Pie, 158

Chocolate-Raspberry Sorbet Sandwiches, 100

Lamb Chops with Tomato–Bell Pepper Salad and Bulgur, 37

Lemon-Pepper Chickpeas, 109

Mexican-Style Beans with Cilantro and Cheese, 112

Mussels in Spicy Tomato Sauce, 123

Pepper and Coriander–Crusted Filet Mignon with Wild Mushrooms, 72

Potato Chip–Coated Sea Bass, 85

Striped Bass with Sweet Pepper Sauce, 42

Szechuan Peanut Noodles, 111

Very Chocolate Rice Pudding, 183

### 6 POINTS value

Baby Plum Cakes, 164

Caprese-Style Perciatelli, 48

Chocolate Fudge Truffle Tart, 193

Crispy Thai Beef Salad with Ginger-Lime Dressing, 73

Falafel Patties with Avocado-Lime Sauce, 87

Ginger-Broiled Salmon with Cucumber-Mint Relish, 124

Grilled Tri-Tip with Chipotle Butter–Slathered Corn, 30

Hoisin Beef and Shiitake Stir-Fry, 116

Horseradish and Panko–Crusted Salmon, 84

Jerk Pork with Grilled Pineapple and Nectarines, 114

Linguine with Cauliflower and Crushed Croutons, 46

New Mexico–Style Green Chile Stew, 115

Penne Arrabbiata, 126

Penne with Asparagus, Ham, and Basil, 34

Pork and Tomato Carnitas, 78

Pressed Cuban Sandwiches, 76

Thai Chicken-Coconut Curry, 121

### 7 POINTS value

Cheesy Enchiladas with Green Sauce, 119

Filet Mignon with Red Chile Onions, 113

Garlicky Chicken Kebabs with Fennel-Spiced Couscous, 35

Golden Phyllo–Topped Turkey Potpie, 83

Peppered Sirloin with Black Bean, Tomato, and Avocado Salad, 32

Summertime Chicken Panzanella Salad, 81

Ziti with Spinach, Tomatoes, and White Beans, 47

### 8 POINTS value

Beef Sliders with Slaw, 74

### 9 POINTS value

Coconut and Curry–Marinated Skewered Chicken, 40

# Recipe Index